INTRODUCTION TO THE STUDY OF MORTUARY CUSTOMS AMONG THE NORTH AMERICAN INDIANS

BY

DR. H. C. YARROW ACT ASST SU G USA

Published by Left of Brain Books

Copyright © 2023 Left of Brain Books

ISBN 978-1-397-66564-5

First Edition

All rights reserved. No part of this publication may be reproduced, distributed, or transmitted in any form or by any means, including photocopying, recording, or other electronic or mechanical methods, without the prior written permission of the publisher, except in the case of brief quotations permitted by copyright law. Left of Brain Books is a division of Left Of Brain Onboarding Pty Ltd.

PUBLISHER'S PREFACE

About the Book

This book details the mortuary customs traditionally used by Native Americans.

CONTENTS

PUBLISHER'S PREFACE
INTRODUCTION 1
INTRODUCTORY 6
    INHUMATION 11
    BURIAL IN CABINS, WIGWAMS, OR HOUSES 19
    STONE GRAVES OR CISTS 21
    BURIAL IN MOUNDS 23
    CHILLICOTHE MOUND 28
    MOUNDS OF STONE 29
    CAVE BURIAL 37
    MUMMIES 42
    URN-BURIAL 53
    SURFACE BURIAL 55
    CAIRN BURIAL 57
    CREMATION 58
    PARTIAL CREMATION 68
    BURIAL ABOVE GROUND 72
    BOX BURIAL 75
    TREE AND SCAFFOLD BURIAL 76
    PARTIAL SCAFFOLD BURIAL AND OSSUARIES 86
    SUPERTERRENE AND AERIAL BURIAL IN CANOES 91
    AQUATIC BURIAL 98
    LIVING SEPULCHERS 100
    MOURNING, FEASTS, FOOD, DANCES, SONGS, GAMES, POSTS, FIRES, AND SUPERSTITIONS IN CONNECTION WITH BURIAL 101
    FINAL REMARKS 117

INTRODUCTION

Washington D. C. July 8, 1880

THIS little volume is the third of a series designed to promote anthropologic researches among the North American Indians. The first was prepared by myself and entitled "Introduction to the Study of Indian Languages," the second by Col. Garrick Mallery entitled Introduc-tion to the Study of Sign Language among the North American Indians.

The following are in course of preparation and will soon appear.

Introduction to the Study of Medicine Practices among the North American Indians

Introduction to the Study of Mythology among the North American Indians

Introduction to the Study of Sociology among the North American Indians

The mortuary customs of savage or barbaric people have a deep signific-ance from the fact that in them are revealed much of the philosophy of the people by whom they are practiced. Early beliefs concerning the nature of human existence in life and after death and the relations of the living to the dead are recorded in these customs. The mystery concerning the future love for the departed who were loved while here, reverence for the wise and good who may after death be wiser and better, hatred and fear of those who were enemies here and may have added powers of enmity in the hereafter--all these and like considerations have led in every tribe to a body of customs of exceeding interest as revealing the opinions, the philosophy of the people themselves.

In these customs, also are recorded evidences of the social condition of the people, the affection in which friends and kindred are held, the very beginnings of altruism in primitive life.

In like manner these customs constitute a record of the moral condition of the people, as in many ways they exhibit the ethic standards by which conduct in human life is judged. For such reasons the study of mortuary customs is of profound interest to the anthropologist.

It is hoped that by this method of research the observations of many men may be brought together and placed on permanent record, and that the body of material may be sufficient, by a careful comparative study, to warrant some general discussion concerning the philosophy of this department of human conduct.

General conclusions can be reached with safety only after materials from many sources have been obtained. It will not be safe for the collector to speculate much upon that which he observes. His own theory or explanation of customs will be of little worth, but the theory and explanation given by the Indians will be of the greatest value. What do the Indians do, and say, and believe? When these are before us it matters little whether our generalizations be true or false. Wiser men may come and use the facts to a truer purpose. It is proposed to make a purely objective study of the Indians, and, as far as possible, to leave the record unmarred by vain subjective speculations.

The student who is pursuing his researches in this field should carefully note all of the customs, superstitions, and opinions of the Indians relating to--

1. The care of the lifeless body prior to burial, much of which he will find elaborated into sacred ceremonies.

2. The method of burial, including the site of burial, the attitude in which the body is placed, and the manner in which it is investured. Here, also, he will find interesting and curious ceremonial observances. The superstitions and opinions of the people relating to these subjects are of importance.

3. The gifts offered to the dead; not only those placed with the body at the time of burial, but those offered at a subsequent time for the benefaction of the departed on his way to the other world, and for his use on arrival. Here, too, it is as important for us to know the ceremonies with which the gifts are made as to know the character of the gifts themselves.

4. An interesting branch of this research relates to the customs of mourning, embracing the time of mourning, the habiliments, the self-mutilations, and other penances, and the ceremonies with which these are accompanied. In all of these cases the reason assigned by the Indians for their doings, their superstitions, and explanations are of prime importance.

5. It is desirable to obtain from the Indians their explanation of human life, their theory of spirits and of the life to come.

A complete account of these customs in any tribe will necessitate the witnessing of many funeral rites, as the custom will differ at the death of different persons, depending upon age, sex, and social standing. To obtain their explanations and superstitions, it will be necessary to interrogate the Indians themselves. This is not an easy task, for the Indians do not talk with freedom about their dead. The awe with which they are inspired, their reverence and love for the departed, and their fear that knowledge which may be communicated may be used to the injury of those whom they have loved, or of themselves, lead them to excessive reticence on these subjects. Their feelings should not be rudely wounded. The better and more thoughtful members of the tribe will at last converse freely on these subjects with those in whom they have learned to place confidence. The stories of ignorant white men and camp attaches should be wholly discarded, and all accounts should be composed of things actually observed, and of relations made by Indians of probity.

This preliminary volume by Dr. H. C Yarrow has been the subject of careful research and of much observation, and will serve in many ways as a hint to the student. The literature of the subject is vast, but to a large extent worthless, from the fact that writers have been hasty travelers or subjective speculators on the matter. It is strange how much of accepted history must be rejected when the statements are carefully criticised and compared with known facts. It has frequently been stated of this or that tribe that mutilations, as the cutting off of fingers and toes, of ears and nose, the pulling out of teeth, &c., are extensively practiced as a mode of mourning find wild scenes of maiming and bloodshed are depicted as following upon the death of a beloved chief or great man yet among these tribes maimed persons are rarely found It is probable that there is some basis of fact for the statement that mutilations are in rare instances practiced among some tribes. But even this qualified statement needs absolute proof.

I am pleased to assure those who will take part in this work by earnest and faithful research that Dr Yarrow will treat them generously by giving them full credit for their work in his final publication.

I must not fail to present my thanks to the Surgeon General of the United States Army and his corps of officers for the interest and assistance they have rendered.

    J W POWELL

WASHINGTON, D C, April 5, 1880

DEAR SIR: I have the honor to offer for your consideration the following paper upon the Mortuary Customs of the North American Indians, and trust it may meet with your approval as an introduction to the study of a subject which, while it has been alluded to by most authors, has received little or no systematic treatment. For this and other reasons I was induced some three years since to commence an examination and collection of data relative to the matter, and the present paper is the outcome of that effort. From the vast amount of material in the Bureau of Ethnology, even at the present time, a large volume might be prepared, but it was thought wiser to endeavor to obtain a still greater array of facts, especially from living observers. If the desired end is attained I shall not count as lost the labor which has been bestowed.

Very respectfully, your obedient servant,

    H C. YARROW.
    Maj. J. W. POWELL,
    In charge of Bureau of Ethnology, Smithsonian Institution

The wisest of beings tells us that it is better to go to the House of Mourning than to that of laughter. And those who have well consider d the grounds he bad for thus his judgment will not by the title of this book (as melancholy as it appears) be affrighted from the perusing it.

What we read to have been and still to be the custom of some nations to make sepulchres the repositories of their greatest riches is (I am sure) universally true in a moral sense however it may be thought in the literal there being never a grave but what conceals a treasure though all have not the art to discover it I do not here invite the covetous miser to disturb the dead who can frame no idea of treasure distinct from gold and silver but him who knows that wisdom and virtue are the true and sole riches of man. Is not truth a treasure think you? Which yet Democritus assures us is buried in a deep pit or grave and he bad reason for whereas we meet elsewhere with nothing but pain and deceit we no sooner look down into a grave but truth faceth us and tells us our own.--MURET

INTRODUCTORY

THE primitive manners and customs of the North American Indians are rapidly passing away under influences of civilization and other disturbing elements. In view of this fact, it becomes the duty of all interested in preserving a record of these customs to labor assiduously, while there is still time, to collect such data as may be obtainable. This seems the more important now, as within the last ten years an almost universal interest has been awakened in ethnologic research, and the desire for more knowledge in this regard is constantly increasing. A wise and liberal government, recognizing the need, has ably seconded the efforts of those engaged in such studies by liberal grants from the public funds; nor is encouragement wanted from the hundreds of scientific societies throughout the civilized globe. The public press, too--the mouth-piece of the people--is ever on the alert to scatter broadcast such items of ethnologic information as its corps of well-trained reporters can secure. To induce further laudable inquiry, and assist all those who may be willing to engage in the good work, is the object of this preliminary work on the mortuary customs of North American Indians, and it is hoped that many more laborers may through it be added to the extensive and honorable list of those who have already contributed.

It would appear that the subject chosen should awaken great interest, since the peculiar methods followed by different nations and the great importance attached to burial ceremonies have formed an almost invariable part of all works relating to the different peoples of our globe; in fact no particular portion of ethnologic research has claimed more attention. In view of these facts, it might seem almost a work of supererogation to continue a further examination of the subject, for nearly every author in writing of our Indian tribes makes some mention of burial observances; but these notices are scattered far and wide on the sea of this special literature, and many of the accounts, unless supported by corroborative evidence, may be considered as entirely unreliable. To bring together and harmonize conflicting statements, and arrange collectively what is known of the subject has been the writer's task, and an enormous mass of information has been acquired, the method of securing which has been as follows:

In the first instance a circular was prepared, which is here given; this at the time was thought to embrace all items relating to the disposal of the dead and attendant ceremonies, although since its distribution other important questions have arisen which will be alluded to subsequently.

"WASHINGTON, D. C, June 15, 1877

"To--

"SIR: Being engaged in preparing a memoir upon the 'Burial Customs of the Indians of North America, both ancient and modern, and the disposal of their dead,' I beg leave to request your kind co-operation to enable me to present as exhaustive an exposition of the subject as possible, and to this end earnestly invite your attention to the following points in regard to which information is desired:

"1st. Name of the tribe

"2d. Locality.

"3d. Manner of burial, ancient and modern.

"4th. Funeral ceremonies.

"5th. Mourning observances, if any.

"With reference to the first of these inquiries, 'Name of the tribe,' the Indian name is desired as well as the name by which the tribe is known to the whites.

"As to 'Locality,' the response should give the range of the tribe, and be full and geographically accurate.

"As to the 'Manner of burial,' &c, it is important to have every particular bearing on this branch of the subject, and much minuteness is desirable.

"For instance:

"(a) Was the body buried in the ground; if so, in what position, and how was the grave prepared and finished?

"(b) If cremated, describe the process, and what disposal was made of the ashes.

"(c) Were any utensils, implements, ornaments, &c., or food placed in the grave? In short, every fact is sought that may possibly add to a general knowledge of the subject.

"Answers to the fourth and fifth queries should give as full and succinct a description as possible of funereal and other mortuary ceremonies at the time of death and subsequently, the period of mourning, manner of its observance, &c.

"In obtaining materials for the purpose in question it is particularly desirable that well-authenticated sources of information only be drawn upon, and, therefore, any points gathered from current rumor or mere hearsay, and upon which there is doubt, should be submitted to searching scrutiny before being embraced in answers to the several interrogatories, and nothing should be recorded as a fact until fully established as such.

"In seeking information from Indians, it is well to remember the great tendency to exaggeration they show, and since absolute facts will alone serve our purpose, great caution is suggested in this particular.

"It is earnestly desired to make the work in question as complete as possible, and therefore it is especially hoped that your response will cover the ground as pointed out by the several questions as thoroughly as you may be able and willing to make it.

"In addition to notes, a reference to published papers either by yourself or others is desirable, as well as the names of those persons who may be able to furnish the needed information.

"Permit me to assure you that, while it is not offered in the way of inducement to secure the service asked, since it is barely possible that you can be otherwise than deeply interested in the extension of the bounds of knowledge, full credit will be given you in the work for whatever information you may be pleased to furnish.

"This material will be published under the auspices of Prof. J.W. Powell, in charge of the U. S Geographical and Geological Survey of the Rocky Mountain Region.

"Communications may be addressed to me either at the address given above or at the Army Medical Museum, Washington, D. C.

"Respectfully, yours,

  "H. C. YARROW."

This was forwarded to every Indian agent, physicians at agencies, to a great number of Army officers who had served or were serving at frontier posts, and to individuals known to be interested in ethnologic matters. A large number of interesting and valuable responses were received, many of them showing how customs have changed either under influences of civilization or altered circumstances of environment.

Following this, a comprehensive list of books relating to North American Indians was procured, and each volume subjected to careful scrutiny, extracts being made from those that appeared in the writer's judgment reliable. Out of a large number examined up to the present time, several hundred have been laid under contribution, and the labor of further collation still continues.

It is proper to add that all the material obtained will eventually be embodied in a quarto volume, forming one of the series of contributions to North American Ethnology prepared under the direction of Maj. J. W. Powell, Director of the Bureau of Ethnology, Smithsonian Institution, from whom, since the inception of the work, most constant encouragement and advice has been received, and to whom all American ethnologists owe a debt of gratitude which can never be repaid.

Having thus called attention to the work and the methods pursued in collecting data, the classification of the subject may be given and examples furnished of the burial ceremonies among different tribes, calling especial attention to similar or almost analogous customs among the peoples of the Old World.

For our present purpose the following provisional arrangement of burials may be adopted:

1st. By INHUMATION in pits, graves, holes in the ground, mounds; cists, and caves.

2d. By CREMATION, generally on the surface of the earth, occasionally beneath, the resulting bones or ashes being placed in pits, in the ground, in boxes placed on scaffolds or trees, in urns, sometimes scattered.

3d. By EMBALMENT or a process of mummifying, the remains being afterwards placed in the earth, caves, mounds, or charnel-houses.

4th. By AERIAL SEPULTURE, the bodies being deposited on scaffolds or trees, in boxes or canoes, the two latter receptacles supported on scaffolds or posts, or on the ground. Occasionally baskets have been used to contain the remains of children, these being hung to trees.

5th. By AQUATIC BURIAL, beneath the water, or in canoes, which were turned adrift.

These heads might, perhaps, be further subdivided, but the above seem sufficient for all practical needs.

The use of the term burial throughout this paper is to be understood in its literal significance, the word being derived from the Anglo-Saxon "birgan," to conceal or hide away.

In giving descriptions of different burials and attendant ceremonies, it has been deemed expedient to introduce entire accounts as furnished, in order to preserve continuity of narrative.

INHUMATION

THE commonest mode of burial among North American Indians has been that of interment in the ground, and this has taken place in a number of different ways; the following will, however, serve as good examples of the process.

"The Mohawks of New York made a large round hole in which the body was placed upright or upon its haunches, after which it was covered with timber, to support the earth which they lay over, and thereby kept the body from being pressed. They then raised the earth in a round hill over it. They always dressed the corpse in all its finery, and put wampum and other things into the grave with it; and the relations suffered not grass nor any weed to grow upon the grave, and frequently visited it and made lamentation." [1]

This account may be found in Schoolcraft.

In Jones [2] is the following interesting account from Lawson, of the burial customs of the Indians formerly inhabiting the Carolinas:

"Among the Carolina tribes, the burial of the dead was accompanied with special ceremonies, the expense and formality attendant upon the funeral according with the rank of the deceased. The corpse was first placed in a cane bundle and deposited in an outhouse made for the purpose, where it was suffered to remain for a day and a night guarded and mourned over by the nearest relatives with disheveled hair. Those who are to officiate at the funeral go into the town, and from the backs of the first young men they meet strip such blankets and matchcoats as they deem suitable for their purpose. In these the dead body is wrapped and then covered with two or three mats made of rushes or cane. The coffin is made of woven reeds or hollow canes tied fast at both ends. When everything is prepared for the interment, the corpse is carried from the house in which it has been lying into the orchard of peach-trees and is there deposited in another bundle.

---

[1] Hist. Indian Tribes of the United States, 1853, part 3, p 183.
[2] Antiq. of Southern Indians, 1873, pp 108-110

Seated upon mats are there congregated the family and tribe of the deceased and invited guests. The medicine man, or conjurer, having enjoined silence, then pronounces a funeral oration, during which he recounts the exploits of the deceased, his valor, skill, love of country, property, and influence, alludes to the void caused by his death, and counsels those who remain to supply his place by following in his footsteps; pictures the happiness he will enjoy in the land of spirits to which he has gone, and concludes his address by an allusion to the prominent traditions of his tribe."

Let us here pause to remind the reader that this custom has prevailed throughout the civilized world up to the present day--a custom, in the opinion of many, "more honored in the breach than the observance."

"At last [says Mr. Lawson], the corpse is brought away from that hurdle to the grave by four young men, attended by the relations, the king, old men, and all the nation. When they come to the sepulchre, which is about six feet deep and eight feet long, having at each end (that is, at the head and foot) a light-wood or pitch-pine fork driven close down the sides of the grave firmly into the ground (these two forks are to contain a ridgepole, as you shall understand presently), before they lay the corpse into the grave, they cover the bottom two or three time over with the bark of trees; then they let down the corpse (with two belts that the Indians carry their burdens withal) very leisurely upon the said barks; then they lay over a pole of the same wood in the two forks, and having a great many pieces of pitch- pine logs about two foot and a half long, they stick them in the sides of the grave down each end and near the top, through of where (sic) the other ends lie in the ridge-pole, so that they are declining like the roof of a house. These being very thick placed, they cover them many times double with bark; then they throw the earth thereon that came out of the grave and beat it down very firm. By this means the dead body lies in a vault, nothing touching him. After a time the body is taken up, the bones cleaned, and deposited in an ossuary called the Quiogozon."

Dr Fordyce Grinnell, physician to the Wichita Agency, Indian Territory, furnishes the following description of the burial ceremonies of the Wichita Indians, who call themselves. "Kitty-la- tats" or those of the tattooed eyelids.

"When a Wichita dies the town-crier goes up and down through the village and announces the fact. Preparations are immediately made for the burial, and the body is taken without delay to the grave prepared for it reception. If the grave is some distance from the village the body is carried thither on the back of a pony, being first wrapped in blankets and then laid prone across the saddle, one walking on either side to support it. The grave is dug from 3 to 4 feet deep and of sufficient length for the extended body. First blankets and buffalo robes are laid in the bottom of the grave, then the body, being taken from the horse and unwrapped, is dressed in its best apparel and with ornaments is placed upon a couch of blankets and robes, with the head towards the west and the feet to the east; the valuables belonging to the deceased are placed with the body in the grave. With the man are deposited his bows and arrows or gun, and with the woman her cooking utensils and other implements of her toil. Over the body sticks are placed six or eight inches deep and grass over these, so that when the earth is filled in it need not come in contact with the body or its trappings. After the grave is filled with earth a pen of poles is built around it, or, as is frequently the case, stakes are driven so that they cross each other from either side about midway over the grave, thus forming a complete protection from the invasion of wild animals. After all this is done, the grass or other debris is carefully scraped from about the grave for several feet, so that the ground is left smooth and clean. It is seldom the case that the relatives accompany the remains to the grave, but they more often employ others to bury the body for them, usually women. Mourning is similar in this tribe as in others, and consists in cutting off the hair, fasting, &c. Horses are also killed at the grave."

The Caddoes, Ascena, or Timber Indians, as they call themselves, follow nearly the same mode of burial as the Wichitas, but one custom prevailing is worthy of mention.

"If a Caddo is killed in battle, the body is never buried, but is left to be devoured by beasts or birds of prey and the condition of such individuals in the other world is considered to be far better than that of persons dying a natural death."

In a work by Bruhier [1] the following remarks, freely translated by the writer, may be found, which note a custom having great similarity to the exposure of bodies to wild beasts mentioned above.

"The ancient Persians threw out the bodies of their dead on the roads, and if they were promptly devoured by wild beasts it was esteemed a great honor, a misfortune if not. Sometimes they interred, always wrapping the dead in a wax cloth to prevent odor."

M. Pierre Muret, [2] from whose book Bruhier probably obtained his information, gives at considerable length an account of this peculiar method of treating the dead among the Persians, as follows:

"It is a matter of astonishment, considering the Persians have ever had the renown of being one of the most civilized Nations in the world, that notwithstanding they should have used such barbarous customs about the Dead as are set down in the Writings of some Historians, and the rather because at this day there are still to be seen among them those remains of Antiquity, which do fully satisfie us, that their Tombs have been very magnificent. And yet nevertheless, if we will give credit to Procopius and Agathias, the Persians were never wont to bury their Dead Bodies, so far were they from bestowing any Funeral Honours upon them. But, as these Authors tell us, they exposed them stark naked in the open fields, which is the greatest shame our Laws do allot to the most infamous Criminals, by laying them open to the view of all upon the highways: Yea, in their opinion it was a great unhappiness, if either Birds or Beasts did not devour their Carcases; and they commonly made an estimate of the Felicity of these poor Bodies, according as they were sooner or later made a prey of. Concerning these, they resolved that they must needs have been very bad indeed, since even the beasts themselves would not touch them; which caused an extream sorrow to their Relations, they taking it for an ill boding to their Family, and an infallible presage of some great misfortune hanging over their heads, for they persuaded themselves, that the Souls which inhabited those Bodies being dragg'd into Hell, would not fail to come and trouble them, and that being always accompanied with the Devils, their Tormentors, they would certainly give them a great deal of disturbance.

---

[1] L'incertitude des Signes de la Mort, 1740, tom 1, p. 430
[2] Rites of Funeral, Ancient and Modern, 1683, p 45

"And on the contrary, when these Corpses were presently devoured, their joy was very great, they enlarged themselves in praises of the Deceased; every one esteeming them undoubtedly happy, and came to congratulate their relations on that account: For as they believed assuredly, that they were entered into the Elysian Fields, so they were persuaded, that they would procure the same bliss for all those of their family.

"They also took a great delight to see Skeletons and Bones scatered up and down in the fields, whereas we can scarcely endure to see those of Horses and Dogs used so. And these remains of Humane Bodies, (the sight whereof gives us so much, horror, that we presently bury them out of our sight, whenever we find them elsewhere than in Charnel- houses or Church yards) were the occasion of their greatest joy because they concluded from thence the happiness of those that had been devoured wishing after then Death to meet with the like good luck."

The same author states and Bruhier corroborates the assertion that the Parthians, Medes, Iberians, Caspians, and a few others had such a horror and aversion of the corruption and decomposition of the dead and of their being eaten by worms that they threw out the bodies into the open fields to be devoured by wild beasts, a part of their belief being that persons so devoured would not be entirely extinct, but enjoy at least a partial sort of life in their living sepulchres. It is quite probable that for these and other reasons the Bactrians and Hircanians trained dogs for this special purpose called Canes sepulchrales which received the greatest care and attention, for it was deemed proper that the souls of the deceased should have strong and lusty frames to dwell in.

George Gibbs [1] gives the following account of burial among the Klamath and Trinity Indians of the Northwest coast.

The graves which are in the immediate vicinity of their houses exhibit very considerable taste and a laudable care. The dead are inclosed in rude coffins formed by placing four boards around the body and covered with earth to some depth; a heavy plank often supported by upright head and foot stones is laid upon the top or stones are built up into a wall about a foot above the ground and the top flagged with others. The graves of the chiefs are surrounded by neat wooden palings, each pale ornamented with

---

[1] Schoolcraft's Hist. Indian Tribes of the United States Pt. 3, 1853, p. 140

a feather from the tail of the bald eagle. Baskets are usually staked down by the side according to the wealth or popularity of the individual and sometimes other articles for ornament or use are suspended over them. The funeral ceremonies occupy three days during which the soul of the deceased is in danger from O-mah- u or the devil. To preserve it from this peril a fire is kept up at the grave and the friends of the deceased howl around it to scare away the demon. Should they not be successful in this the soul is carried down the river, subject, however, to redemption by Peh-ho wan on payment of a big knife. After the expiration of three days it is all well with them.

The question may well be asked, is the big knife a "sop to Cerberus"?

Capt. F. E. Grossman, [1] USA, furnishes the following account of burial among the Pimas of Arizona:

"The Pimas tie the bodies of their dead with ropes, passing the latter around the neck and under the knees and then drawing them tight until the body is doubled up and forced into a sitting position. They dig the grave from four to five feet deep and perfectly round (about two feet in diameter), then hollow out to one side of the bottom of this grave a sort of vault large enough to contain the body. Here the body is deposited, the grave is filled up level with the ground, and poles, trees, or pieces of timber placed upon the grave to protect the remains from the coyotes (a species of wolf). Burials usually take place at night, without much ceremony. The mourners chant during the burial, but signs of grief are rare. The bodies of their dead are buried, if possible, immediately after death has taken place, and the graves are generally prepared before the patients die. Sometimes sick persons (for whom the graves had already been dug) recovered; in such cases the graves are left open until the persons for whom they were intended die. Open graves of this kind can be seen in several of their burial-grounds. Places of burial are selected some distance from the village, and, if possible, in a grove of mesquite bushes. Immediately after the remains have been buried, the house and personal effects of the deceased are burned, and his horses and cattle killed, the meat being cooked as a repast for the mourners. The nearest relatives of the deceased, as a sign of their sorrow, remain in the village for weeks and sometimes months; the men

---

[1] Rep. Smithson. Inst., 1871, p. 414

cut off about six inches of their long hair, while the women cut their hair quite short"

The Coyotero Apaches, according to Dr. W. J. Hoffman, [1] in disposing of their dead, seem to be actuated by the desire to spare themselves any needless trouble, and prepare the defunct and the grave in this manner.

"The Coyoteros, upon the death of a member of the tribe, partially wrap up the corpse and deposit it into the cavity left by the removal of a small rock or the stump of a tree. After the body has been crammed into the smallest possible space the rock or stump is again rolled into its former position, when a number of stones are placed around the base to keep out the coyotes. The nearest of kin usually mourn for the period of one month, during that time giving utterance at intervals to the most dismal lamentations, which are apparently sincere. During the day this obligation is frequently neglected or forgotten, but when the mourner is reminded of his duty he renews his howling with evident interest. This custom of mourning for the period of thirty days corresponds to that formerly observed by the Natchez."

Somewhat similar to this rude mode of sepulture is that described in the life of Moses Van Campen, which relates to the Indians formerly inhabiting Pennsylvania:

"Directly after the Indians proceeded to bury those who had fallen in battle, which they did by rolling an old log from its place and laying the body in the hollow thus made, and then heaping upon it a little earth"

As a somewhat curious, if not exceptional, interment, the following account, relating to the Indians of New York is furnished, by Mr. Franklin B. Hough, who has extracted it from an unpublished journal of the agents of a French company kept in 1794:

"Saw Indian graves on the plateau of Independence Rock. The Indians plant a stake on the right side of the head of the deceased and bury them in a bark canoe. Their children come every year to bring provisions to the place where their fathers are buried. One of the graves had fallen in and we observed in the soil some sticks for stretching skins, the remains of a

---

[1] U.S. Geol. Surv. of Terr. for 1876, p. 473

canoe, &c., and the two straps for carrying it, and near the place where the head lay were the traces of a fire which they had kindled for the soul of the deceased to come and warm itself by and to partake of the food deposited near it.

"These were probably the Massasauga Indians, then inhabiting the north shore of Lake Ontario, but who were rather intruders here, the country being claimed by the Oneidas."

It is not to be denied that the use of canoes for coffins has occasionally been remarked, for the writer in 1875 removed from the graves at Santa Barbara an entire skeleton which was discovered in a redwood canoe, but it is thought that the individual may have been a noted fisherman, particularly as the implements of his vocation--nets, fish-spears, &c.--were near him, and this burial was only an exemplification of the well-rooted belief common to all Indians, that the spirit in the next world makes use of the same articles as were employed in this one. It should be added that of the many hundreds of skeletons uncovered at Santa Barbara the one mentioned presented the only example of the kind.

Among the Indians of the Mosquito coast, in Central America, canoe burial in the ground, according to Bancroft[1], was common, and is thus described:

"The corpse is wrapped in cloth and placed in one-half of a pitpan which has been cut in two. Friends assemble for the funeral and drown their grief in mushla, the women giving vent to their sorrow by dashing themselves on the ground until covered with blood, and inflicting other tortures, occasionally even committing suicide. As it is supposed that the evil spirit seeks to obtain possession of the body, musicians are called in to lull it to sleep while preparations are made for its removal. All at once four naked men, who have disguised themselves with paint so as not to be recognized and punished by Wulasha, rush out from a neighboring hut, and, seizing a rope attached to the canoe, drag it into the woods, followed by the music and the crowd. Here the pitpan is lowered into the grave with bow, arrow, spear, paddle, and other implements to serve the departed in the land beyond, then the other half of the boat is placed over the body. A rude hut is constructed over the grave, serving as a receptacle for the choice food, drink, and other articles placed there from time to time by relatives."

---

[1] Native Races of Pacific States, 1874, vol. 1, p 744.

BURIAL IN CABINS, WIGWAMS, OR HOUSES

WHILE there is a certain degree of similitude between the above-noted methods and the one to be mentioned subsequently--lodge burial--they differ, inasmuch as the latter are examples of surface or aerial burial, and must consequently fall under another caption. The narratives which are now to be given afford a clear idea of the former kind of burial.

Bartram [1] relates the following regarding the Muscogulges of the Carolinas:

"The Muscogulges bury their deceased in the earth; they dig a four- foot, square, deep pit under the cabin, or couch which the deceased laid on in his house, lining the grave with cypress bark, when they place the corpse in a sitting posture, as if it were alive, depositing with him his gun, tomahawk, pipe, and such other matters as he had the greatest value for in his lifetime. His eldest wife, or the queen dowager, has the second choice of his possessions, and the remaining effects are divided among his other wives and children."

According to Bernard Roman, the "funeral customs of the Chickasaws did not differ materially from those of the Muscogulges. They interred the dead as soon as the breath left the body, and beneath the couch in which the deceased expired."

The Navajos of New Mexico and Arizona, a tribe living a considerable distance from the Chickasaws, follow somewhat similar customs, as related by Dr. John Menard, formerly a physician to their agency.

"The Navajo custom is to leave the body where it dies, closing up the house or hogan or covering the body with stones or brush. In case the body is removed, it is taken to a cleft in the rocks and thrown in, and stones piled over. The person touching or carrying the body, first takes off all his clothes and afterwards washes his body with water before putting them on or

---

[1] Bartram's Travels, 1791, pp. 515.

mingling with the living. When a body is removed from a house or hogan, the hogan is burned down, and the place in every case abandoned, as the belief is that the devil comes to the place of death and remains where a dead body is. Wild animals frequently (indeed, generally) get the bodies, and it is a very easy matter to pick up skulls and bones around old camping grounds, or where the dead are laid. In case it is not desirable to abandon a place, the sick person is left out in some lone spot protected by brush, where they are either abandoned to their fate or food brought to them until they die. This is done only when all hope is gone. I have found bodies thus left so well inclosed with brush that wild animals were unable to get at them; and one so left to die was revived by a cup of coffee from our house and is still living and well."

Mr. J. L. Burchard, agent to the Round Valley Indians of California, furnishes an account of burial somewhat resembling that of the Navajos:

"When I first came here the Indians would dig a round hole in the ground, draw up the knees of the deceased Indian, and wrap the body into as small a bulk as possible in blankets, tie them firmly with cords, place them in the grave, throw in beads, baskets, clothing, everything owned by the deceased, and often donating much extra; all gathered around the grave wailing most pitifully, tearing their faces with their nails till the blood would run down their cheeks, pull out their hair, and such other heathenish conduct. These burials were generally made under their thatch houses or very near thereto. The house where one died was always torn down, removed, rebuilt, or abandoned. The wailing, talks, &c., were in their own jargon; none else could understand, and they seemingly knew but little of its meaning (if there was any meaning in it); it simply seemed to be the promptings of grief, without sufficient intelligence to direct any ceremony; each seemed to act out his own impulse"

STONE GRAVES OR CISTS

THESE are of considerable interest, not only from their somewhat rare occurrence, except in certain localities, but from the manifest care taken by the survivors to provide for the dead what they considered a suitable resting-place. A number of cists have been found in Tennessee, and are thus described by Moses Fiske: [1]

"There are many burying grounds in West Tennessee with regular graves. They dug them 12 or 18 inches deep, placed slabs at the bottom ends and sides, forming a kind of stone coffin, and, after laying in the body, covered it over with earth."

It may be added that, in 1873, the writer assisted at the opening of a number of graves of men of the reindeer period, near Solutre, in France, and they were almost identical in construction with those described by Mr. Fiske, with the exception that the latter were deeper; this, however, may be accounted for if it is considered how great a deposition of earth may have taken place during the many centuries which have elapsed since the burial. Many of the graves explored by the writer in 1875, at Santa Barbara, resembled somewhat cist graves, the bottom and sides of the pit being lined with large flat stones, but there were none directly over the skeletons.

The next account is by Maj. J. W. Powell, the result of his observation in Tennessee. "These ancient cemeteries are exceedingly abundant throughout the State, often hundreds of graves may be found on a single hillside. In some places the graves are scattered and in others collected in mounds, each mound being composed of a large number of cist graves. It is evident that the mounds were not constructed at one time, but the whole collection of graves therein was made during long periods by the addition of a new grave from time to time. In the first burials found at the bottom and near the center of a mound a tendency to a concentric system, with the feet inward, is observed, and additions are made around and above

---

[1] Trans. Amer. Antiq. Soc., 1820 vol. 1, p. 302

these first concentric graves, as the mound increases in size the burials become more and more irregular:

"Some other peculiarities are of interest. A larger number of interments exhibit the fact that the bodies were placed there before the decay of the flesh, while in other cases collections of bones are buried. Sometimes these bones were placed in some order about the crania, and sometimes in irregular piles, as if the collection of bones had been emptied from a sack. With men, pipes, stone hammers, knives, arrowheads, &c., were usually found; with women, pottery, rude beads, shells, &c.; with children, toys of pottery, beads, curious pebbles, &c.

"Sometimes, in the subsequent burials, the side slab of a previous burial was used as a portion of the second cist. All of the cists were covered with slabs."

Dr. Jones has given an exceedingly interesting account of the stone graves of Tennessee, in his volume published by the Smithsonian Institution, to which valuable work [1] the reader is referred for a more detailed account of this mode of burial.

---

[1] Antiquities of Tennessee, Cont. to Knowledge, Smith. Inst., 1876, No. 259, 4 deg., pp. 1, 8, 37, 52, 55, 82.

BURIAL IN MOUNDS

IN view of the fact that the subject of mound-burial is so extensive, and that in all probability a volume by a member of the Bureau of Ethnology may shortly be published, it is not deemed advisable to devote any considerable space to it in this paper, but a few interesting examples may be noted to serve as indications to future observers.

The first to which attention is directed is interesting as resembling cist-burial combined with deposition in mounds. The communication is from Prof. F. W. Putnam, curator of the Peabody Museum of Archaology, Cambridge, made to the Boston Society of Natural History, and is published in volume XX of its proceedings, October 15, 1878:

"...He then stated that it would be of interest to the members, in connection with the discovery of dolmens in Japan, as described by Professor Morse, to know that within twenty-four hours there had been received at the Peabody Museum a small collection of articles taken from rude dolmens (or chambered barrows, as they would be called in England), recently opened by Mr. E. Curtiss, who is now engaged, under his direction, in exploration for the Peabody Museum.

"These chambered mounds are situated in the eastern part of Clay County, Missouri, and form a large group on both sides of the Missouri River. The chambers are, in the three opened by Mr. Curtiss, about 8 feet square, and from 4-1/2 to 5 feet high, each chamber having a passage-way several feet in length and 2 in width leading from the southern side and opening on the edge of the mound formed by covering the chamber and passage-way with earth. The walls of the chambered passages were about 2 feet thick, vertical, and well made of stones, which were evenly laid without clay or mortar of any kind. The top of one of the chambers had a covering of large, flat rocks, but the others seem to have been closed over with wood. The chambers were filled with clay which had been burnt, and appeared as if it had fallen in from above. The inside walls of the chambers also showed signs of fire. Under the burnt clay, in each chamber, were found the remains of several human skeletons, all of which had been burnt to such an extent as to leave but small fragments of the bones, which were mixed with the ashes and charcoal. Mr. Curtiss thought that in one chamber he found the remains of 5 skeletons and in another 13. With these skeletons there were a few flint implements and minute fragments of vessels of clay.

"A large mound near the chambered mounds was also opened, but in this no chambers were found. Neither had the bodies been burnt. This mound proved remarkably rich in large flint implements, and also contained well-made pottery and a peculiar "gorget" of red stone. The connection of the people who placed the ashes of their dead in the stone chambers with those who buried their dead in the earth mounds is, of course, yet to be determined."

It is quite possible, indeed probable, that these chambers were used for secondary burials, the bodies having first been cremated.

In the volume of the proceedings already quoted the same investigator gives an account of other chambered mounds which are, like the preceding, very interesting, the more so as adults only were inhumed therein, children having been buried beneath the dwelling-floors:

"Mr. F. W. Putnam occupied the rest of the evening with an account of his explorations of the ancient mounds and burial places in the Cumberland Valley, Tennessee.

"The excavations had been carried on by himself, assisted by Mr. Edwin Curtiss, for over two years, for the benefit of the Peabody Museum at Cambridge. During this time many mounds of various kinds had been thoroughly explored, and several thousand of the singular stone graves of the mound builders of Tennessee had been carefully opened.... Mr. Putnam's remarks were illustrated by drawings of several hundred objects obtained from the graves and mounds, particularly to show the great variety of articles of pottery and several large and many unique forms of implements of chipped flint. He also exhibited and explained in detail a map of a walled town of this old nation. This town was situated on the Lindsley estate, in a bend of Spring Creek. The earth embankment, with its accompanying ditch, encircled an area of about 12 acres. Within this inclosure there was one large mound with a flat top, 15 feet high, 130 feet long, and 90 feet wide, which was found not to be a burial mound. Another mound near the large one, about 50 feet in diameter, and only a few feet high, contained 60 human skeletons, each in a carefully-made stone grave, the graves being arranged in two rows, forming the four sides of a square, and in three layers.... The most important discovery lie made within the inclosure was that of finding the remains of the houses of the people who lived in this old town. Of them about 70 were traced out and located on the map by Professor Buchanan, of Lebanon, who made the survey for Mr. Putnam. Under the floors of hard clay, which was in places much burnt, Mr. Putnam found the graves of children. As only the bodies of adults had been placed in the one mound devoted to burial, and as nearly every site of a house he explored had from one to four graves of children under the clay floor, he was convinced that it was a regular custom to bury the children in that way. He also found that the children had been undoubtedly treated with affection, as in their small graves were found many of the best pieces of pottery he obtained, and also quantities of shell-beads, several large pearls, and many other objects which were probably the playthings of the little ones while living." [1]

This cist mode of burial is by no means uncommon in Tennessee, as they are frequently mentioned by writers on North American archaeology.

The examples which follow are specially characteristic, some of them serving to add strength to the theory that mounds were for the most part used for secondary burial, although intrusions were doubtless common.

Of the burial mounds of Ohio, Caleb Atwater [2] gives this description.

"Near the center of the round fort ... was a tumulus of earth about 10 feet in height and several rods in diameter at its base. On its eastern side, and extending six rods from it, was a semicircular pavement composed of pebbles such as are now found in the bed of the Scioto River, from whence they appear to have been brought. The summit of this tumulus was nearly 30 feet in diameter, and there was a raised way to it, leading from the east, like a modern turnpike. The summit was level. The outline of the semicircular pavement and the walk is still discernible. The earth composing this mound was entirely removed several years since. The writer was present at its removal and carefully examined the contents. It contained--

---

[1] A detailed account of this exploration, with many illustrations, will be found in the Eleventh Annual Report of the Peabody Museum, Cambridge, 1878.
[2] Trans. Amer. Antiq. Soc., 1820, i, p. 174 et seq.

"1st. Two human skeletons lying on what had been the original surface of the earth.

"2d. A great quantity of arrow-heads, some of which were so large as to induce a belief that they were used as spear-heads.

"3d. The handle either of a small sword or a large knife, made of an elk's horn. Around the end where the blade had been inserted was a ferule of silver, which, though black, was not much injured by time. Though the handle showed the hole where the blade had been inserted, yet no iron was found, but an oxyde remained of similar shape and size.

"4th. Charcoal and wood ashes on which these articles lay, which were surrounded by several bricks very well burnt. The skeleton appeared to have been burned in a large and very hot fire, which had almost consumed the bones of the deceased. This skeleton was deposited a little to the south of the center of the tumulus; and about 20 feet to the north of it was another, with which were--

"5th. A large mirrour about 3 feet in breadth and 1-1/2 inches in thickness This mirrour was of isinglass (mica membranacea), and on it--

"6th. A plate of iron which had become an oxyde, but before it was disturbed by the spade resembled a plate of cast iron. The mirrour answered the purpose very well for which it was intended. This skeleton had also been burned like the former, and lay on charcoal and a considerable quantity of wood ashes. A part of the mirrour is in my possession, as well as a piece of brick taken from the spot at the time. The knife or sword handle was sent to Mr. Peal's Museum at Philadelphia.

"To the southwest of this tumulus, about 40 rods from it, is another, more than 90 feet in height, which is shown on the plate representing these works. It stands on a large hill, which appears to be artificial. This must have been the common cemetery, as it contains an immense number of human skeletons of all sizes and ages. The skeletons are laid horizontally, with their heads generally towards the center and the feet towards the outside of the tumulus. A considerable part of this work still stands uninjured, except by time. In it have been found, besides these skeletons, stone axes and knives and several ornaments, with holes through them, by means of which, with a cord passing through these perforations they could be worn by their owners. On the south side of this tumulus, and not far from it, was a semicircular fosse, which, when I first saw it, was 6 feet deep. On opening it was discovered at the bottom a great quantity of human bones, which I am inclined to believe were the remains of those who had been slain in some great and destructive battle first, because they belonged to persons who had attained their full size, whereas in the mound adjoining were found the skeletons of persons of all ages, and, secondly, they were here in the utmost confusion, as if buried in a hurry. May we not conjecture that they belonged to the people who resided in the town, and who were victorious in the engagement? Otherwise they would not have been thus honorably buried in the common cemetery."

CHILLICOTHE MOUND

"Its perpendicular height was about 15 feet, and the diameter of its base about 60 feet. It was composed of sand and contained human bones belonging to skeletons which were buried in different parts of it. It was not until this pile of earth was removed and the original surface exposed to view that a probable conjecture of its original design could be formed. About 20 feet square of the surface had been leveled and covered with bark. On the center of this lay a human skeleton, over which had been spread a mat manufactured either from weeds or bark. On the breast lay what had been a piece of copper, in the form of a cross, which had now become verdigrise. On the breast also lay a stone ornament with two perforations, one near each end, through which passed a string, by means of which it was suspended around the wearer's neck. On this string, which was made of sinews, and very much injured by time, were placed a great many heads made of ivory or bone, for I cannot certainly say which...."

MOUNDS OF STONE

"Two such mounds have been described already in the county of Perry. Others have been found in various parts of the country. There is one at least in the vicinity of Licking River, not many miles from Newark. There is another on a branch of Hargus's Creek, a few miles to the northeast of Circleville. There were several not very far from the town of Chillicothe. If these mounds were sometimes used as cemeteries of distinguished persons, they were also used as monuments with a view of perpetuating the recollection of some great transaction or event. In the former not more generally than one or two skeletons are found; in the latter none. These mounds are like those of earth, in form of a cone, composed of small stones on which no marks of tools were visible. In them some of the most interesting articles are found, such as urns, ornaments of copper, heads of spears, &c., of the same metal, as well as medals of copper and pickaxes of horneblende; ... works of this class, compared with those of earth, are few, and they are none of them as large as the mounds at Grave Creek, in the town of Circleville, which belong to the first class. I saw one of these stone tumuli which had been piled on the surface of the earth on the spot where three skeletons had been buried in stone coffins, beneath the surface. It was situated on the western edge of the hill on which the "walled town" stood, on Paint Creek. The graves appear to have been dug to about the depth of ours in the present times. After the bottom and sides were lined with thin flat stones, the corpses were placed in these graves in an eastern and western direction, and large flat stones were laid over the graves; then the earth which had been dug out of the graves was thrown over them. A huge pile of stones was placed over the whole. It is quite probable, however, that this was a work of our present race of Indians. Such graves are more common in Kentucky than Ohio. No article, except the skeletons, was found in these graves; and the skeletons resembled very much the present race of Indians."

The mounds of Sterling County, Illinois, are described by W. C. Holbrook, [1] as follows:

---

[1] Amer. Natural, 1877, xi, No. 11, p. 688

"I recently made an, examination of a few of the many Indian mounds found on Rock River, about two miles above Sterling, Ill. The first one opened was an oval mound about 20 feet long, 12 feet wide, and 7 feet high. In the interior of this I found a dolmen or quadrilateral wall about 10 feet long, 4 feet high, and 4-1/2 feet wide. It had been built of lime-rock from a quarry near by, and was covered with large flat stones No mortar or cement had been used. The whole structure rested on the surface of the natural soil, the interior of which had been scooped out to enlarge the chamber. Inside of the dolmen I found the partly decayed remains of eight human skeletons, two very large teeth of an unknown animal, two fossils, one of which is not found in this place, and a plummet. One of the long bones had been splintered; the fragments had united, but there remained large morbid growths of bone (exostosis) in several places. One of the skulls presented a circular opening about the size of a silver dime. This perforation had been made during life, for the edges had commenced to cicatrize. I later examined three circular mounds, but in them I found no dolmens. The first mound contained three adult human skeletons, a few fragments of the skeleton of a child, the lower maxillary of which indicated it to be about six years old. I also found claws of some carnivorous animal. The surface of the soil had been scooped out and the bodies laid in the excavation and covered with about a foot of earth, fires had then been made upon the grave and the mound afterwards completed. The bones had not been charred. No charcoal was found among the bones, but occurred in abundance in a stratum about one foot above them. Two other mounds, examined at the same time, contained no remains.

"Of two other mounds, opened later, the first was circular, about 4 feet high, and 15 feet in diameter at the base, and was situated on an elevated point of land close to the bank of the river. From the top of this mound one might view the country for many miles in almost any direction. On its summit was an oval altar 6 feet long and 4-1/2 wide. It was composed of flat pieces of limestone, which had been burned red, some portions having been almost converted into lime. On and about this altar I found abundance of charcoal. At the sides of the altar were fragments of human bones, some of which had been charred. It was covered by a natural growth of vegetable mold and sod, the thickness of which was about 10 inches. Large trees had once grown in this vegetable mold, but their stumps were so decayed I could not tell with certainty to what species they belonged. Another large mound was opened which contained nothing."

The next account relates to the grave-mounds near Pensacola, Fla., and was originally published by Dr. George M. Sternberg, surgeon United States Army. [1]

"Before visiting the mound I was informed that the Indians were buried in it in an upright position, each one with a clay pot on his head. This idea was based upon some superficial explorations which had been made from time to time by curiosity hunters. Their excavations had, indeed, brought to light pots containing fragments of skulls, but not buried in the position they imagined. Very extensive explorations made at different times by myself have shown that only fragments of skulls and of the long bones of the body are to be found in the mound, and that these are commonly associated with earthen pots, sometimes whole, but more frequently broken fragments only. In some instances portions of the skull were placed in a pot, and the long bones were deposited in its immediate vicinity. Again, the pots would contain only sand, and fragments of bones would be found near them. The most successful 'find' I made was a whole nest of pots, to the number of half a dozen, all in a good state of preservation, and buried with a fragment of skull, which I take from its small size to have been that of a female. Whether this female was thus distinguished above all others buried in the mound by the number of pots deposited with her remains because of her skill in the manufacture of such ware, or by reason of the unusual wealth of her sorrowing husband, must remain a matter of conjecture. I found altogether fragments of skulls and thigh-bones belonging to at least fifty individuals, but in no instance did I find anything like a complete skeleton. There were no vertebra, no ribs, no pelvic bones, and none of the small bones of the hands and feet. Two or three skulls nearly perfect were found, but they were so fragile that it was impossible to preserve them. In the majority of instances only fragments of the frontal and parietal bones were found, buried in pots or in fragments of pots too small to have ever contained a complete skull. The conclusion was irresistible that this was not a burial- place for the bodies of deceased Indians, but that the bones had been gathered from some other locality for burial in this mound, or that cremation was practiced before burial, and the fragments of bone not consumed by fire were gathered and deposited in the mound. That the latter supposition is the correct one I deem probable from the fact that in digging in the mound evidences of fire are found in numerous places, but without any regularity as to depth and position. These evidences consist in

---

[1] Proc. Am. Ass. Adv. of Science, 1875, p. 288

strata of from one to four inches in thickness, in which the sand is of a dark color and has mixed with it numerous small fragments of charcoal.

"My theory is that the mound was built by gradual accretion in the following manner. That when a death occurred a funeral pyre was erected on the mound, upon which the body was placed. That after the body was consumed, any fragments of bones remaining were gathered, placed in a pot, and buried, and that the ashes and cinders were covered by a layer of sand brought from the immediate vicinity for that purpose. This view is further supported by the fact that only the shafts of the long bones are found, the expanded extremities, which would be most easily consumed, having disappeared; also, by the fact that no bones of children were found. Their bones being smaller, and containing a less proportion of earthy matter, would be entirely consumed....

"At the Santa Rosa mound the method of burial was different. Here I found the skeletons complete, and obtained nine well-preserved skulls.... The bodies were not apparently deposited upon any regular system, and I found no objects of interest associated with the remains. It may be that this was due to the fact that the skeletons found were those of warriors who had fallen in battle in which they had sustained a defeat. This view is supported by the fact that they were all males, and that two of the skulls bore marks of ante-mortem injuries which must have been of a fatal character."

Writing of the Choctaws, Bartram, [1]in alluding to the ossuary or bone-house, mentions that so soon as this is filled a general inhumation takes place, in this manner.

"Then the respective coffins are borne by the nearest relatives of the deceased to the place of interment, where they are all piled one upon another in the form of a pyramid, and the conical hill of earth heaped above. The funeral ceremonies are concluded with the solemnization of a festival called the feast of the dead."

Mr. Florian Gianque, of Cincinnati, Ohio, furnishes an account of a somewhat curious mound burial which had taken place in the Miami Valley of Ohio.

---

[1] Bartram's Travels, 1791, p. 513.

"A mound was opened in this locality, some years ago, containing a central corpse in a sitting posture, and over thirty skeletons buried around it in a circle, also in a sitting posture but leaning against one another, tipped over towards the right facing inwards. I did not see this opened, but have seen the mounds and many ornaments, awls, &c., said to have been found near the central body. The parties informing me are trustworthy."

As an example of interment, unique, so far as known, and interesting as being sui generis, the following is presented, with the statement that the author, Dr J. Mason Spainhour, of Lenoir, N.C., bears the reputation of an observer of undoubted integrity, whose facts as given may not be doubted.

"Excavation of an Indian mound by J. Mason Spainhour, D.D.S., of Lenoir, Caldwell County, North Carolina, March 11, 1871, on the farm of R. V. Michaux, esq., near John's River, in Burke County, North Carolina"

"In a conversation with Mr. Michaux on Indian curiosities, he informed me that there was an Indian mound on his farm which was formerly of considerable height, but had gradually been plowed down, that several mounds in the neighborhood had been excavated and nothing of interest found in them. I asked permission to examine this mound, which was granted, and upon investigation the following facts were revealed.

"Upon reaching the place, I sharpened a stick 4 or 5 feet in length and ran it down in the earth at several places, and finally struck a rock about 18 inches below the surface, which, on digging down, was found to be smooth on top, lying horizontally upon solid earth, about 18 inches above the bottom of the grave, 18 inches in length, and 16 inches in width, and from 2 to 3 inches in thickness, with the corners rounded.

"Not finding anything under this rock, I then made an excavation in the south of the grave, and soon struck another rock, which upon examination proved to be in front of the remains of a human skeleton in a sitting posture. The bones of the fingers of the right hand were resting on this rock, and on the rock near the hand was a small stone about 5 inches long, resembling a tomahawk or Indian hatchet. Upon a further examination many of the bones were found, though in a very decomposed condition, and upon exposure to the air soon crumbled to pieces. The heads of the bones, a considerable portion of the skull, maxillary bones, teeth, neck bones, and the vertebra, were in their proper places, though the weight of the earth above them had driven them down, yet the entire frame was so perfect that it was an easy matter to trace all the bones; the bones of the cranium were slightly inclined toward the east. Around the neck were found coarse beads that seemed to be of some hard substance and resembled chalk. A small lump of red paint about the size of an egg was found near the right side of this skeleton. The sutures of the cranium indicated the subject to have been 25 or 28 years of age, and its top rested about 12 inches below the mark of the plow.

"I made a further excavation toward the west of this grave and found another skeleton, similar to the first, in a sitting posture, facing the east. A rock was on the right, on which the bones of the right hand were resting, and on this rock was a tomahawk which had been about 7 inches in length, but was broken into two pieces, and was much better finished than the first. Beads were also around the neck of this one, but are much smaller and of finer quality than those on the neck of the first. The material, however, seems to be the same. A much larger amount of paint was found by the side of this than the first. The bones indicated a person of large frame, who, I think, was about 50 years of age. Everything about this one had the appearance of superiority over the first. The top of the skull was about 6 inches below the mark of the plane.

"I continued the examination, and, after diligent search, found nothing at the north side of the grave; but, on reaching the east, found another skeleton, in the same posture as the others, facing the west. On the right side of this was a rock on which the bones of the right hand were resting, and on the rock was also a tomahawk, which had been about 8 inches in length, but was broken into three pieces, and was composed of much better material, and better finished than the others. Beads were also found on the neck of this, but much smaller and finer than those of the others. A larger amount of paint than both of the others was found near this one. The top of the cranium had been moved by the plow. The bones indicated a person of 40 years of age.

"There was no appearance of hair discovered; besides, the smaller bones were almost entirely decomposed, and would crumble when taken from their bed in the earth. These two circumstances, coupled with the fact that the farm on which this grave was found was the first settled in that part of the country, the date of the first deed made from Lord Granville to John Perkins running back about 150 years (the land still belonging to the descendants of the same family that first occupied it), would prove beyond doubt that it is a very old grave.

"The grave was situated due east and west, in size about 9 by 6 feet, the line being distinctly marked by the difference in the color of the soil. It was dug in rich, black loam, and filled around the bodies with white or yellow sand, which I suppose was carried from the river- bank, 200 yards distant. The skeletons approximated the walls of the grave, and contiguous to them was a dark-colored earth, and so decidedly different was this from all surrounding it, both in quality and odor, that the line of the bodies could be readily traced. The odor of this decomposed earth, which had been flesh, was similar to clotted blood, and would adhere in lumps when compressed in the hand.

"This was not the grave of the Indian warriors; in those we find pots made of earth or stone, and all the implements of war, for the warrior had an idea that after he arose from the dead he would need, in the 'hunting-grounds beyond,' his bow and arrow, war-hatchet, and scalping-knife.

"The facts set forth will doubtless convince every Mason who will carefully read the account of this remarkable burial that the American Indians were in possession of at least some of the mysteries of our order, and that it was evidently the grave of Masons, and the three highest officers in a Masonic lodge. The grave was situated due east and west; an altar was erected in the center; the south, west, and east were occupied--the north was not; implements of authority were near each body. The difference in the quality of the beads, the tomahawks in one, two, and three pieces, and the difference that the bodies were placed from the surface, indicate beyond doubt that these three persons had been buried by Masons, and those, too, that understood what they were doing.

"Will some learned Mason unravel this mystery, and inform the Masonic world how they obtained so much Masonic information?

"The tomahawks, maxillary bones, some of the teeth, beads, and other bones, have been forwarded to the Smithsonian Institution at Washington, D.C., to be placed among the archives of that institution for exhibition, at which place they may be seen."

If Dr. Spainhour's inferences are incorrect, still there is a remarkable coincidence of circumstances patent to every Mason.

CAVE BURIAL

NATURAL or artificial holes in the ground, caverns, and fissures in rocks have been used as places of deposit for the dead since the earliest periods of time, and are used up to the present day by not only the American Indians, but by peoples noted for their mental elevation and civilization, our cemeteries furnishing numerous specimens of artificial or partly artificial caves. As to the motives which have actuated this mode of burial, a discussion would be out of place at this time, except as may incidentally relate to our own Indians, who, so far as can be ascertained, simply adopted caves as ready and convenient resting places for their deceased relatives and friends.

In almost every State in the Union burial caves have been discovered, but as there is more or less of identity between them, a few illustrations will serve the purpose of calling the attention of observers to the subject.

While in the Territory of Utah, in 1872, the writer discovered a natural cave not far from the House Range of mountains, the entrance to which resembled the shaft of a mine. In this the Gosi-Ute Indians had deposited their dead, surrounded with different articles, until it was quite filled up; at least it so appeared from the cursory examination made, limited time preventing a careful exploration. In the fall of the same year another cave was heard of, from an Indian guide, near the Nevada border, in the same Territory, and an attempt made to explore it, which failed for reasons to be subsequently given. This Indian, a Gosi-Ute, who was questioned regarding the funeral ceremonies of his tribe, informed the writer that not far from the very spot where the party were encamped was a large cave in which he had himself assisted in placing dead members of his tribe. He described it in detail and drew a rough diagram of its position and appearance within. He was asked if an entrance could be effected, and replied that he thought not, as some years previous his people had stopped up the narrow entrance to prevent game from seeking a refuge in its vast vaults, for he asserted that it was so large and extended so far under ground that no man knew its full extent. In consideration, however, of a very liberal bribe, after many refusals, he agreed to act as guide. A rough ride of over an hour and the desired spot was reached. It was found to be almost upon the apex of a small mountain apparently of volcanic origin, for the hole which was pointed out appeared to have been the vent of the crater. This entrance was irregularly circular in form and descended at an angle. As the Indian had stated, it was completely stopped up with large stones and roots of sage brush, and it was only after six hours of uninterrupted, faithful labor that the attempt to explore was abandoned. The guide was asked if many bodies were therein, and replied "Heaps, heaps," moving the hands upwards as far as they could be stretched. There is no reason to doubt the accuracy of the information received, as it was voluntarily imparted.

In a communication received from Dr. A. J McDonald, physician to the Los Pinos Indian Agency, Colorado, a description is given of crevice or rock-fissure burial, which follows.

"As soon as death takes place the event is at once announced by the medicine-man, and without loss of time the squaws are busily engaged in preparing the corpse for the grave. This does not take long; whatever articles of clothing may have been on the body at the time of death are not removed. The dead man's limbs are straightened out, his weapons of war laid by his side, and his robes and blankets wrapped securely and snugly around him, and now everything is ready for burial. It is the custom to secure, if possible, for the purpose of wrapping up the corpse, the robes and blankets in which the Indian died. At the same time that the body is being fitted for interment, the squaws having immediate care of it, together with all the other squaws in the neighborhood, keep up a continued chant or dirge, the dismal cadence of which may, when the congregation of women is large, be heard for quite a long distance. The death song is not a mere inarticulate howl of distress; it embraces expressions eulogistic in character, but whether or not any particular formula of words is adopted on such occasion is a question which I am unable, with the materials at my disposal, to determine with any degree of certainty.

"The next duty falling to the lot of the squaws is that of placing the dead man on a horse and conducting the remains to the spot chosen for burial. This is in the cleft of a rock, and, so far as can be ascertained, it has always been customary among the Utes to select sepulchres of this character. From descriptions given by Mr. Harris, who has several times been fortunate enough to discover remains, it would appear that no superstitious ideas are held by this tribe with respect to the position in which the body is placed, the space accommodation of the sepulchre probably regulating this matter; and from the same source I learn that it is not usual to find the remains of more than one Indian deposited in one grave. After the body has been received into the cleft, it is well covered with pieces of rock, to protect it against the ravages of wild animals. The chant ceases, the squaws disperse, and the burial ceremonies are at an end. The men during all this time have not been idle, though they have in no way participated in the preparation of the body, have not joined the squaws in chanting praises to the memory of the dead, and have not even as mere spectators attended the funeral, yet they have had their duties to perform. In conformity with a long-established custom, all the personal property of the deceased is immediately destroyed. His horses and his cattle are shot, and his wigwam, furniture, &c., burned. The performance of this part of the ceremonies is assigned to the men; a duty quite in accord with their taste and inclinations. Occasionally the destruction of horses and other property is of considerable magnitude, but usually this is not the case, owing to a practice existing with them of distributing their property among their children while they are of a very tender age, retaining to themselves only what is necessary to meet every-day requirements.

"The widow 'goes into mourning' by smearing her face with a substance composed of pitch and charcoal. The application is made but once, and is allowed to remain on until it wears off. This is the only mourning observance of which I have any knowledge.

"The ceremonies observed on the death of a female are the same as those in the case of a male, except that no destruction of property takes place, and of course no weapons are deposited with the corpse. Should a youth die while under the superintendence of white men, the Indians will not as a rule have anything to do with the interment of the body. In a case of the kind which occurred at this agency some time ago, the squaws prepared the body in the usual manner; the men of the tribe selected a spot for the burial, and the employes at the agency, after digging a grave and depositing the corpse therein, filled it up according to the fashion of civilized people, and then at the request of the Indians rolled large fragments of rocks on top. Great anxiety was exhibited by the Indians to have the employes perform the service as expeditiously as possible."

An interesting cave in Calaveras County, California, which had been used for burial purposes, is thus described by Prof. J. D. Whitney: [1]

"The following is an account of the cave from which the skulls, now in the Smithsonian collection, were taken. It is near the Stanislaus River, in Calaveras County, on a nameless creek, about two miles from Abbey's Ferry, on the road to Vallicito, at the house of Mr. Robinson. There were two or three persons with me, who had been to the place before and knew that the skulls in question were taken from it. Their visit was some ten years ago, and since that the condition of things in the cave has greatly changed. Owing to some alteration in the road, mining operations, or some other cause which I could not ascertain, there has accumulated on the formerly clean stalagmitic floor of the cave a thickness of some 20 feet of surface earth that completely conceals the bottom, and which could not be removed without considerable expense. This cave is about 27 feet deep at the mouth and 40 to 50 feet at the end, and perhaps 30 feet in diameter. It is the general opinion of those who have noticed this cave and saw it years ago that it was a burying-place of the present Indians. Dr. Jones said he found remains of bows and arrows and charcoal with the skulls he obtained, and which were destroyed at the time the village of Murphy's was burned. All the people spoke of the skulls as lying on the surface and not as buried in the stalagmite."

The next description of cave burial, described by W. H. Dall[2], is so remarkable that it seems worthy of admittance to this paper. It relates probably to the Innuit of Alaska.

"The earliest remains of man found in Alaska up to the time of writing I refer to this epoch [Echinus layer of Dall]. There are some crania found by us in the lowermost part of the Amaknak cave and a cranium obtained at Adakh, near the anchorage in the Bay of Islands. These were deposited in a remarkable manner, precisely similar to that adopted by most of the continental Innuit, but equally different from the modern Aleut fashion. At the Amaknak cave we found what at first appeared to be a wooden inclosure, but which proved to be made of the very much decayed supra-maxillary bones of some large cetacean. These were arranged so as to form a rude rectangular inclosure covered over with similar pieces of bone. This

---

[1] Rep. Smithsonian Inst. 1867, p. 406.
[2] Contrib. to N. A. Ethnol., 1877, vol 1, p 62.

was somewhat less than 4 feet long, 2 feet wide, and 18 inches deep. The bottom was formed of flat pieces of stone. Three such were found close together, covered with and filled by an accumulation of fine vegetable and organic mold. In each was the remains of a skeleton in the last stages of decay. It had evidently been tied up in the Innuit fashion to get it into its narrow house, but all the bones, with the exception of the skull, were reduced to a soft paste, or even entirely gone. At Adakh a fancy prompted me to dig into a small knoll near the ancient shell-heap; and here we found, in a precisely similar sarcophagus, the remains of a skeleton, of which also only the cranium retained sufficient consistency to admit of preservation. This inclosure, however, was filled with a dense peaty mass not reduced to mold, the result of centuries of sphagnous growth, which had reached a thickness of nearly 2 feet above the remains. When we reflect upon the well-known slowness of this kind of growth in these northern regions, attested by numerous Arctic travelers, the antiquity of the remains becomes evident."

It seems beyond doubt that in the majority of cases, especially as regards the caves of the Western States and Territories, the interments were primary ones, and this is likewise true of many of the caverns of Ohio, Indiana, and Kentucky, for in the three States mentioned many mummies have been found, but it is also likely that such receptacles were largely used as places of secondary deposits. The many fragmentary skeletons and loose bones found seem to strengthen this view.

MUMMIES

IN connection with cave burial, the subject of mummifying or embalming the dead may be taken up, as most specimens of the kind have generally been found in such repositories.

It might be both interesting and instructive to search out and discuss the causes which have led many nations or tribes to adopt certain processes with a view to prevent that return to dust which all flesh must sooner or later experience, but the necessarily limited scope of this preliminary work precludes more than a brief mention of certain theories advanced by writers of note, and which relate to the ancient Egyptians. Possibly at the time the Indians of America sought to preserve their dead from decomposition some such ideas may have animated them, but on this point no definite information has been procured. In the final volume an effort will be made to trace out the origin of mummification among the Indians and aborigines of this continent.

The Egyptians embalmed, according to Cassien, because during the time of the annual inundation no interments could take place, but it is more than likely that this hypothesis is entirely fanciful. It is said by others they believed that so long as the body was preserved from corruption the soul remained in it. Herodotus states that it was to prevent bodies from becoming a prey to animal voracity. "They did not inter them," says he, "for fear of their being eaten by worms; nor did they burn, considering fire as a ferocious beast, devouring everything which it touched." According to Diodorus of Sicily, embalmment originated in filial piety and respect. De Maillet, however, in his tenth letter on Egypt, attributes it entirely to a religious belief insisted upon by the wise men and priests, who taught their disciples that after a certain number of cycles, of perhaps thirty or forty thousand years, the entire universe became as it was at birth, and the souls of the dead returned into the same bodies in which they had lived, provided that the body remained free from corruption, and that sacrifices were freely offered as oblations to the manes of the deceased. Considering the great care taken to preserve the dead, and the ponderously solid nature of their tombs, it is quite evident that this theory obtained many believers among the people. M. Gannal believes embalmment to have been suggested by the affectionate sentiments of our nature--a desire to preserve as long as possible the mortal remains of loved ones; but MM. Volney and Pariaet think it was intended to obviate, in hot climates especially, danger from pestilence, being primarily a cheap and simple process, elegance and luxury coming later; and the Count de Caylus states the idea of embalmment was derived from the finding of desiccated bodies which the burning sands of Egypt had hardened and preserved. Many other suppositions have arisen, but it is thought the few given above are sufficient to serve as an introduction to embalmment in North America.

From the statements of the older writers on North American Indians, it appears that mummifying was resorted to among certain tribes of Virginia, the Carolinas, and Florida, especially for people of distinction, the process in Virginia for the kings, according to Beverly, [1]being as follows:

"The Indians are religious in preserving the Corpses of their Kings and Rulers after Death, which they order in the following manner: First, they neatly flay off the Skin as entire as they can, slitting it only in the Back; then they pick all the Flesh off from the Bones as clean as possible, leaving the Sinews fastned to the Bones, that they may preserve the Joints together: then they dry the Bones in the Sun, and put them into the Skin again, which in the mean time has been kept from drying or shrinking; when the Bones are placed right in the Skin, they nicely fill up the Vacuities, with a very fine white Sand. After this they sew up the Skin again, and the Body looks as if the Flesh had not been removed. They take care to keep the Skin from shrinking, by the help of a little Oil or Grease, which saves it also from Corruption. The Skin being thus prepar'd, they lay it in an apartment for that purpose, upon a large Shelf rais'd above the Floor. This Shelf is spread with Mats, for the Corpse to rest easy on, and skreened with the same, to keep it from the Dust. The Flesh they lay upon Hurdles in the Sun to dry, and when it is thoroughly dried, it is sewed up in a Basket, and set at the Feet of the Corpse, to which it belongs. In this place also they set up a Quioccos, or Idol, which they believe will be a Guard to the Corpse. Here Night and Day one or other of the Priests must give his Attendance, to take care of the dead Bodies. So great an Honour and Veneration have these ignorant and unpolisht People for their Princes even after they are dead."

---

[1] Hist. of Virginia, 1722, p 185

It should be added that, in the writer's opinion, this account and others like it are somewhat apocryphal, and it has been copied and recopied a score of times.

According to Pinkerton[1], the Werowanco preserved their dead as follows:

"... By him is commonly the sepulchre of their Kings. Their bodies are first bowelled, then dried upon hurdles till they be very dry, and so about the most of their joints and neck they hang bracelets, or chains of copper, pearl, and such like, as they used to wear. Their inwards they stuff with copper beads, hatchets, and such trash. Then lap they them very carefully in white skins, and so roll them in mats for their winding-sheets. And in the tomb, which is an arch made of mats, they lay them orderly. What remaineth of this kind of wealth their Kings have, they set at their feet in baskets. These temples and bodies are kept by their priests.

"For their ordinary burials, they dig a deep hole in the earth with sharp stakes, and the corpse being lapped in skins and mats with their jewels they lay them upon sticks in the ground, and so cover them with earth. The burial ended, the women being painted all their faces with black coal and oil do sit twenty-four hours in the houses mourning and lamenting by turns with such yelling and howling as may express their great passions....

"Upon the top of certain red sandy hills in the woods there are three great houses filled with images of their Kings and devils and tombs of their predecessors. Those houses are near sixty feet in length, built harbourwise after their building. This place they count so holy as that but the priests and Kings dare come into them; nor the savages dare not go up the river in boats by it, but they solemnly cast some piece of copper, white beads, or pocones into the river for fear their Okee should be offended and revenged of them.

"They think that their Werowances and priests which they also esteem quiyoughcosughs, when they are dead do go beyond the mountains towards the setting of the sun, and ever remain there in form of their Okee, with their heads painted red with oil and pocones, finely trimmed with feathers, and shall have beads, hatchets, copper, and tobacco, doing nothing but dance and sing with all their predecessors. But the common

---

[1] Collection of Voyages, 1812, vol. XIII, p 39.

people they suppose shall not live after death, but rot in their graves like dead dogs."

The remark regarding truthfulness will apply to this account in common with the former.

The Congaree or Santee Indians of South Carolina, according to Lawson, used a process of partial embalmment, as will be seen from the subjoined extract from Schoolcraft; [1] but instead of laying away the remains in caves, placed them in boxes supported above the ground by crotched sticks.

"The manner of their interment is thus: A mole or pyramid of earth is raised, the mould thereof being worked very smooth and even, sometimes higher or lower, according to the dignity of the person whose monument it is. On the top thereof is an umbrella, made ridgeways, like the roof of a house. This is supported by nine stakes or small posts, the grave being about 6 or 8 feet in length and 4 feet in breadth, about which is hung gourds, feathers, and other such like trophies, placed there by the dead man's relations in respect to him in the grave. The other parts of the funeral rites are thus: As soon as the party is dead they lay the corpse upon a piece of bark in the sun, seasoning or embalming it with a small root beaten to powder, which looks as red as vermilion; the same is mixed with bear's oil to beautify the hair. After the carcass has laid a day or two in the sun they remove it and lay it upon crotches cut on purpose for the support thereof from the earth then they anoint it all over with the aforementioned ingredients of the powder of this root and bear's oil. When it is so done they cover it over very exactly with the bark of the pine or cypress tree to prevent any rain to fall upon it, sweeping the ground very clean all about it. Some of his nearest of kin brings all the temporal estate he was possessed of at his death, as guns, bows and arrows, beads, feathers, match coat etc. This relation is the chief mourner, being clad in moss, with a stick in his hand, keeping a mournful ditty for three or four days, his face being black with the smoke of pitch pine mixed with bear's oil. All the while he tells the dead mans relations and the rest of the spectators who that dead person was, and of the great feats performed in his lifetime, all that he speaks tending to the praise of the defunct. As soon as the flesh grows mellow and will cleave from the bone they get it off and burn it, making the bones very clean then anoint them with the ingredients aforesaid, wrapping up the

---

[1] Hist. Indian Tribes of the United States, 1854, Part IV, p. 155, et seq

skull (very carefully) in a cloth artificially woven of opossum's hair. The bones they carefully preserve in a wooden box, every year oiling and cleansing them. By these means they preserve them for many ages that you may see an Indian in possession of the bones of his grandfather or some of his relations of a longer antiquity. They have other sorts of tombs as when an Indian is slain in, that very place they make a heap of stones (or sticks where stones are not to be found), to this memorial every Indian that passes by adds a stone to augment the heap in respect to the deceased hero. The Indians make a roof of light wood or pitch pine over the graves of the more distinguished, covering it with bark and then with earth leaving the body thus in a subterranean vault until the flesh quits the bones. The bones are then taken up, cleaned, jointed, clad in white dressed deer skins, and laid away in the Quiogozon, which is the royal tomb or burial place of their kings and war captains, being a more magnificent cabin reared at the public expense. This Quiogozon is an object of veneration, in which the writer says he has known the king, old men, and conjurers to spend several days with their idols and dead kings, and into which he could never gain admittance."

Another class of mummies are those which have been found in the saltpeter and other caves of Kentucky, and it is still a matter of doubt with archaeologists whether any special pains were taken to preserve these bodies, many believing that the impregnation of the soil with certain minerals would account for the condition in which the specimens were found. Charles Wilkins [1] thus describes one:

"... exsiccated body of a female ... was found at the depth of about 10 feet from the surface of the cave bedded in clay strongly impregnated with nitre, placed in a sitting posture, incased in broad stones standing on their edges, with a flat stone covering the whole. It was enveloped in coarse clothes, ... the whole wrapped in deer- skins, the hair of which was shaved off in the manner in which the Indians prepare them for market. Enclosed in the stone coffin were the working utensils, beads, feathers, and other ornaments of dress which belonged to her."

The next description is by Dr Samuel L. Mitchill: [2]

---

[1] Trans. Amer. Antiq. Soc., 1820, vol. 1, p. 360
[2] Trans. and Coll. Amer. Antiq. Soc., 1820, vol. 1, p. 318

[A letter from Dr. Mitchill of New York, to Samuel M. Burnside, Esq., Secretary of the American Antiquarian Society, on North American Antiquities.]

"Aug 24th, 1815

"DEAR SIR: I offer you some observations on a curious piece of American antiquity now in New York, It is a human body [1] found in one of the limestone caverns of Kentucky. It is a perfect exsiccation, all the fluids are dried up. The skin, bones, and other firm parts are in a state of entire preservation. I think it enough to have puzzled Bryant and all the archaologists.

"This was found in exploring a calcareous cave in the neighborhood of Glasgow for saltpetre.

"These recesses, though under ground, are yet dry enough to attract and retain the nitrick acid. It combines with lime and potash, and probably the earthy matter of these excavations contains a good proportion of calcareous carbonate. Amidst these drying and antiseptick ingredients, it may be conceived that putrefaction would be stayed, and the solids preserved from decay. The outer envelope of the body is a deer skin, probably dried in the usual way and perhaps softened before its application by rubbing. The next covering is a deer's skin, whose hair had been cut away by a sharp instrument resembling a hatter's knife. The remnant of the hair and the gashes in the skin nearly resemble a sheared pelt of beaver. The next wrapper is of cloth made of twine doubled and twisted. But the thread does not appear to have been formed by the wheel, nor the web by the loom. The warp and filling seem to have been crossed and knotted by an operation like that of the fabricks of the northwest coast, and of the Sandwich islands. Such a botanist as the lamented Muhlenburgh could determine the plant which furnished the fibrous material.

"The innermost tegument is a mantle of cloth like the preceding, but furnished with large brown feathers arranged and fastened with great art

---

[1] A mummy of this kind, of a person of mature age, discovered in Kentucky, is now in the cabinet of the American Antiquarian Society. It is a female. Several human bodies were found enwrapped carefully in skins and cloths. They were inhumed below the floor of the cave, inhumed, and not lodged in catacombs.

so as to be capable of guarding the living wearer from wet and cold. The plumage is distinct and entire, and the whole bears a near similitude to the feathery cloaks now worn by the nations of the northwestern coast of America. A Wilson might tell from what bird they were derived.

"The body is in a squatting posture with the right arm reclining forward and its hand encircling the right leg. The left arm hangs down, with its hand inclined partly under the seat. The individual, who was a male did not probably exceed the age of fourteen, at his death. There is near the occiput a deep and extensive fracture of the skull, which probably killed him. The skin has sustained little injury, it is of a dusky colour, but the natural hue cannot be decided with exactness from its present appearance. The scalp, with small exceptions is cohered with sorrel or foxy hair. The teeth are white and sound. The hands and feet, in their shrivelled state, are slender and delicate. All this is worthy the investigation of our acute and perspicacious colleague, Dr Holmes.

"There is nothing bituminous or aromatic in or about the body, like the Egyptian mummies, nor are there bandages around any part. Except the several wrappers, the body is totally naked. There is no sign of a suture or incision about the belly whence it seems that the viscera were not removed.

"It may now be expected that I should offer some opinion, as to the antiquity and race of this singular exsiccation.

"First, then, I am satisfied that it does not belong to that class of white men of which we are members.

"2dly. Nor do I believe that it ought to be referred to the bands of Spanish adventurers, who, between the years 1500 and 1600, rambled up the Mississippi, and along its tributary streams. But on this head I should like to know the opinion of my learned and sagacious friend, Noah Webster.

"3dly. I am equally obliged to reject the opinion that it belonged to any of the tribes of aborigines, now or lately inhabiting Kentucky.

"4thly. The mantle of the feathered work, and the mantle of twisted threads, so nearly resemble the fabricks of the indigines of Wakash and the Pacifick islands, that I refer this individual to that era of time, and that generation of men, which preceded the Indians of the Green River, and of the place where these relicks were found. This conclusion is strengthened by the consideration that such manufactures are not prepared by the actual and resident red men of the present day. If the Abbe Clavigero had had this case before him, he would have thought of the people who constructed those ancient forts and mounds, whose exact history no man living can give. But I forbear to enlarge; my intention being merely to manifest my respect to the society for having enrolled me among its members, and to invite the attention of its Antiquarians to further inquiry on a subject of such curiosity.

"With respect, I remain yours,

"SAMUEL L. MITCHILL"

It would appear from recent researches on the Northwest coast that the natives of that region embalmed their dead with much care, as may be seen from the work recently published by W. H. Dall, [1] the description of the mummies being as follows:

"We found the dead disposed of in various ways; first, by interment in their compartments of the communal dwelling, as already described; second, by being laid on a rude platform of drift-wood or stones in some convenient rock shelter. These lay on straw and moss, covered by matting, and rarely have either implements, weapons, or carvings associated with them. We found only three or four specimens in all in these places, of which we examined a great number. This was apparently the more ancient form of disposing of the dead, and one which more recently was still pursued in the case of poor or unpopular individuals.

"Lastly, in comparatively modern times, probably within a few centuries, and up to the historic period (1740), another mode was adopted for the wealthy, popular, or more distinguished class. The bodies were eviscerated, cleansed from fatty matters in running water, dried, and usually placed in suitable cases in wrappings of fur and fine grass matting The body was usually doubled up into the smallest compass, and the mummy case, especially in the case of children, was usually suspended (so as not to touch the ground) in some convenient rock shelter. Sometimes, however, the

---

[1] Cont. to N. A. Ethnol., 1877, vol. 1, p. 89

prepared body was placed in a lifelike position, dressed and armed. They were placed as if engaged in some congenial occupation, such as hunting, fishing, sewing, etc. With them were also placed effigies of the animals they were pursuing, while the hunter was dressed in his wooden armor and provided with an enormous mask, all ornamented with feathers and a countless variety of wooden pendants, colored in gay patterns. All the carvings were of wood, the weapons even were only fac-similes in wood of the original articles. Among the articles represented were drums, rattles, dishes, weapons, effigies of men, birds, fish, and animals, wooden armor of rods or scales of wood, and remarkable masks, so arranged that the wearer when erect could only see the ground at his feet. These were worn at their religious dances from an idea that a spirit which was supposed to animate a temporary idol was fatal to whoever might look upon it while so occupied. An extension of the same idea led to the masking of those who had gone into the land of spirits.

"The practice of preserving the bodies of those belonging to the whaling class--a custom peculiar to the Kadiak Innuit--has erroneously been confounded with the one now described. The latter included women as well as men, and all those whom the living desired particularly to honor. The whalers, however, only preserved the bodies of males, and they were not associated with the paraphernalia of those I have described. Indeed, the observations I have been able to make show the bodies of the whalers to have been preserved with stone weapons and actual utensils instead of effigies, and with the meanest apparel, and no carvings of consequence. These details, and those of many other customs and usages of which the shell heaps bear no testimony ... do not come within my line."

Martin Sauer, secretary to Billings' Expedition [1] in 1802, speaks of the Aleutian Islanders embalming their dead, as follows:

"They pay respect, however, to the memory of the dead, for they embalm the bodies of the men with dried moss and grass; bury them in their best attire, in a sitting posture, in a strong box, with their darts and instruments; and decorate the tomb with various coloured mats, embroidery, and paintings. With women, indeed, they use less ceremony. A mother will keep a dead child thus embalmed in their hut for some months, constantly

---

[1] Billings' Exped. 1802, p. 167.

wiping it dry; and they bury it when it begins to smell, or when they get reconciled to parting with it."

Regarding these same people, a writer in the San Francisco Bulletin gives this account-

"The schooner William Sutton, belonging to the Alaska Commercial Company, has arrived from the seal islands of the company with the mummified remains of Indians who lived on an island north of Ounalaska one hundred and fifty years ago. This contribution to science was secured by Captain Henning, an agent of the company, who has long resided at Ounalaska. In his transactions with the Indians he learned that tradition among the Aleuts assigned Kagamale, the island in question, as the last resting-place of a great chief, known as Karkhayahouchak. Last year the captain was in the neighborhood of Kagamale, in quest of sea-otter and other furs and he bore up for the island, with the intention of testing the truth of the tradition he had heard. He had more difficulty in entering the cave than in finding it, his schooner having to beat on and off shore for three days. Finally, he succeeded in effecting a landing, and clambering up the rocks he found himself in the presence of the dead chief, his family and relatives.

"The cave smelt strongly of hot sulphurous vapors. With great care the mummies were removed, and all the little trinkets and ornaments scattered around were also taken away.

"In all there are eleven packages of bodies. Only two or three have as yet been opened. The body of the chief is inclosed in a large basket-like structure, about four feet in height. Outside the wrappings are finely-wrought sea-grass matting, exquisitely close in texture, and skins. At the bottom is a broad hoop or basket of thinly-cut wood, and adjoining the center portions are pieces of body armor composed of reeds bound together. The body is covered with the fine skin of the sea-otter, always a mark of distinction in the interments of the Aleuts, and round the whole package are stretched the meshes of a fish-net, made of the sinews of the sea lion; also those of a bird-net. There are evidently some bulky articles inclosed with the chief's body, and the whole package differs very much from the others, which more resemble, in their brown-grass matting, consignments of crude sugar from the Sandwich Islands than the remains of human beings. The bodies of a pappoose and of a very little child, which probably died at birth or soon after it, have sea-otter skins around them. One of the feet of the latter projects, with a toe-nail visible. The remaining mummies are of adults.

"One of the packages has been opened, and it reveals a man's body in tolerable preservation, but with a large portion of the face decomposed. This and the other bodies were doubled up at death by severing some of the muscles at the hip and knee joints and bending the limbs downward horizontally upon the trunk. Perhaps the most peculiar package, next to that of the chief, is one which incloses in a single matting, with sea-lion skins, the bodies of a man and woman. The collection also embraces a couple of skulls, male and female, which have still the hair attached to the scalp. The hair has changed its color to a brownish red. The relics obtained with the bodies include a few wooden vessels scooped out smoothly; a piece of dark, greenish, flat stone, harder than the emerald, which the Indians use to tan skins; a scalp-lock of jet-black hair; a small rude figure, which may have been a very ugly doll or an idol; two or three tiny carvings in ivory of the sea-lion, very neatly executed, a comb, a necklet made of birds' claws inserted into one another, and several specimens of little bags, and a cap plaited out of sea-grass and almost water-tight."

With the foregoing examples as illustration, the matter of embalmment may be for the present dismissed, with the advice to observers that particular care should be taken, in case mummies are discovered, to ascertain whether the bodies have been submitted to a regular preservative process, or owe their protection to ingredients in the soil of their graves or to desiccation in arid districts.

URN-BURIAL

TO close the subject of subterranean burial proper, the following account of urn-burial in Foster [1] may be added:

"Urn-burial appears to have been practiced to some extent by the mound-builders, particularly in some of the Southern States. In the mounds on the Wateree River, near Camden, S. C., according to Dr. Blanding, ranges of vases, one above the other, filled with human remains, were found. Sometimes when the mouth of the vase is small the skull is placed with the face downward in the opening, constituting a sort of cover. Entire cemeteries have been found in which urn-burial alone seems to have been practiced. Such a one was accidentally discovered not many years since in Saint Catherine's Island, on the coast of Georgia. Professor Swallow informs me that from a mound at New Madrid, Mo, he obtained a human skull inclosed in an earthen jar, the lips of which were too small to admit of its extraction. It must therefore have been molded on the head after death."

"A similar mode of burial was practiced by the Chaldeans, where the funeral jars often contain a human cranium much too expanded to admit of the possibility of its passing out of it, so that either the clay must have been modeled over the corpse, and then baked, or the neck of the jar must have been added subsequently to the other rites of interment." [2]

It is with regret that the writer feels obliged to differ from the distinguished author of the work quoted regarding urn-burial, for notwithstanding that it has been employed by some of the Central and Southern American tribes, it is not believed to have been customary, but to a very limited extent, in North America, except as a secondary interment. He must admit that he himself has found bones in urns or ollas in the graves of New Mexico and California, but under circumstances that would seem to indicate a deposition long subsequent to death. In the graves of the ancient peoples of California a number of ollas were found in long-used burying places, and it is probable that as the bones were dug up time and again for new burials

---

[1] Pre-Historic Races, 1873, p. 199
[2] Rawlinson's Herodotus, Book 1, chap 198, note.

they were simply tossed into pots, which were convenient receptacles, or it may have been that bodies were allowed to repose in the earth long enough for the fleshy parts to decay, and the bones were then collected, placed in urns, and reinterred. Dr. E. Foreman, of the Smithsonian Institution, furnishes the following account of urns used for burial:

"I would call your attention to an earthenware burial-urn and cover, Nos. 27976 and 27977, National Museum, but very recently received from Mr. William McKinley, of Milledgeville, Ga. It was exhumed on his plantation, ten miles below that city, on the bottom lands of the Oconee River, now covered with almost impassable canebrakes, tall grasses, and briers. We had a few months ago from the same source one of the covers, of which the ornamentation was different but more entire. A portion of a similar cover has been received also from Chattanooga, Ga. Mr. McKinley ascribes the use of these urns and covers to the Muscogees, a branch of the Creek Nation."

These urns are made of baked clay, and are shaped somewhat like the ordinary steatite ollas found in the California coast graves, but the bottoms instead of being round run down to a sharp apex; on the top was a cover, the upper part of which also terminated in an apex, and around the border, near where it rested on the edge of the vessel, are indented scroll ornamentations.

The burial-urns of New Mexico are thus described by E. A. Barber: [1]

"Burial-urns ... comprise vessels or ollas without handles, for cremation, usually being from 10 to 15 inches in height, with broad, open mouths, and made of coarse clay, with a laminated exterior (partially or entirely ornamented). Frequently the indentations extend simply around the neck or rim, the lower portion being plain."

So far as is known, up to the present time no burial-urns have been found in North America resembling those discovered in Nicaragua by Dr. J. C. Bransford, U. S. N., but it is quite within the range of possibility that future researches in regions not far distant from that which he explored may reveal similar treasures.

---

[1] Amer. Natural, 1876, vol X, p. 455 et seq

SURFACE BURIAL

THIS mode of interment was practiced to only a limited extent, so far as can be discovered, and it is quite probable that in most cases it was employed as a temporary expedient when the survivors were pressed for time. The Seminoles of Florida are said to have buried in hollow trees, the bodies being placed in an upright position, occasionally the dead being crammed into a hollow log lying on the ground. With some of the Eastern tribes a log was split in half and hollowed out sufficiently large to contain the corpse; it was then lashed together with withes and permitted to remain where it was originally placed. In some cases a pen was built over and around it. This statement is corroborated by Mr. R. S. Robertson, of Fort Wayne, Ind., who states in a communication received in 1877 that the Miamis practiced surface burial in two different ways:

"... 1st. The surface burial in hollow logs. These have been found in heavy forests. Sometimes a tree has been split and the two halves hollowed out to receive the body, when it was either closed with withes or confined to the ground with crossed stakes; and sometimes a hollow tree is used by closing the ends.

"2d. Surface burial where the body was covered by a small pen of logs laid up as we build a cabin, but drawing in every course until they meet in a single log at the top."

Romantically conceived, and carried out to the fullest possible extent in accordance with the ante mortem wishes of the dead, were the obsequies of Blackbird, the great chief of the Omahas. The account is given by George Catlin: [1]

"He requested them to take his body down the river to this his favorite haunt, and on the pinnacle of this towering bluff to bury him on the back of his favorite war-horse, which was to be buried alive under him, from whence he could see, as he said, 'the Frenchmen passing up and down the

---

[1] Manners, Customs, &c., of North American Indiana, 1844, vol. ii, p. 5

river in their boats.' He owned, amongst many homes, a noble white steed, that was led to the top of the grass- covered hill, and with great pomp and ceremony, in the presence of the whole nation and several of the far-traders and the Indian agent, he was placed astride of his horse's back, with his bow in his hand, and his shield and quiver slung, with his pipe and his medicine bag, with his supply of dried meat, and his tobacco-pouch replenished to last him through the journey to the beautiful hunting grounds of the shades of his fathers, with his flint and steel and his tinder to light his pipes by the way; the scalps he had taken from his enemies' heads could be trophies for nobody else, and were hung to the bridle of his horse. He was in full dress, and fully equipped, and on his head waved to the last moment his beautiful head-dress of the war-eagles' plumes. In this plight, and the last funeral honors having been performed by the medicine-men, every warrior of his band painted the palm and fingers of his right hand with vermilion, which was stamped and perfectly impressed on the milk-white sides of his devoted horse. This all done, turfs were brought and placed around the feet and legs of the horse, and gradually laid up to its sides, and at last over the back and head of the unsuspecting animal, and last of all over the head and even the eagle plumes of its valiant rider, where all together have smouldered and remained undisturbed to the present day."

CAIRN BURIAL

THE next mode of interment to be considered is that of cairn or rock burial, which has prevailed and is still common to a considerable extent among the tribes living in the Rocky Mountains and the Sierra Nevadas.

In the summer of 1872 the writer visited one of these rock cemeteries in middle Utah, which had been used for a period not exceeding fifteen or twenty years. It was situated at the bottom of a rock slide, upon the side of an almost inaccessible mountain, in a position so carefully chosen for concealment that it would have been almost impossible to find it without a guide. Several of the graves were opened and found to have been constructed in the following manner: A number of bowlders had been removed from the bed of the slide until a sufficient cavity had been obtained; this was lined with skins, the corpse placed therein, with weapons, ornaments, etc., and covered over with saplings of the mountain aspen; on top of these the removed bowlders were piled, forming a huge cairn, which appeared large enough to have marked the last resting place of an elephant. In the immediate vicinity of the graves were scattered the osseous remains of a number of horses which had been sacrificed no doubt during the funeral ceremonies. In one of the graves, said to contain the body of a chief, in addition to a number of articles useful and ornamental, were found parts of the skeleton of a boy, and tradition states that a captive boy was buried alive at this place.

In connection with this mode of burial it may be said that the ancient Balearic Islanders covered their dead with a heap of stones, but this ceremony was preceded by an operation which consisted in cutting the body in small pieces and collecting in a pot.

CREMATION

NEXT should be noted this mode of disposing of the dead, a common custom to a considerable extent among North American tribes, especially those living on the western slope of the Rocky Moun-tains, although we have undoubted evidence that it was also practiced among the more eastern ones. This rite may be considered as peculiarly interesting from its great antiquity, for Tegg informs us that it reached as far back as the Theban war, in the account of which mention is made of the burning of Menoaeus and Archemorus, who were contemporary with Jair, eighth judge of Israel. It was common in the interior of Asia and among the ancient Greeks and Romans, and has also prevailed among the Hindoos up to the present time. In fact, it is now rapidly becoming a custom among civilized people.

While there is a certain degree of similarity between the performance of this rite among the peoples spoken of and the Indians of North America, yet, did space admit, a discussion might profitably be entered upon regarding the details of it among the ancients and the origin of the ceremony. As it is, simple narrations of cremation in this country, with discursive notes and an account of its origin among the Nishinams of California, by Stephen Powers, [1] seem to be all that is required at this time.

"The moon and the coyote wrought together in creating all things that exist. The moon was good, but the coyote was bad. In making men and women the moon wished to so fashion their souls that when they died they should return to the earth after two or three days, as he himself does when he dies. But the coyote was evil disposed, and said this should not be, but that when men died their friends should burn their bodies, and once a year make a great mourning for them, and the coyote prevailed. So, presently when a deer died, they burned his body, as the coyote had decreed, and after a year they made a great mourning for him. But the moon created the rattlesnake and caused it to bite the coyote's son, so that he died. Now, though the coyote had been willing to burn the deer's relations, he refused to burn his own son. Then the moon said unto him, 'This is your own rule.

---

[1] Cont. to N. A. Ethnol., 1877, vol. iii, p. 341

You would have it so, and now your son shall be burned like the others.' So he was burned, and after a year the coyote mourned for him. Thus the law was established over the coyote also, and, as he had dominion over men, it prevailed over men likewise.

"This story is utterly worthless for itself, but it has its value in that it shows there was a time when the California Indians did not practice cremation, which is also established by other traditions. It hints at the additional fact that the Nishinams to this day set great store by the moon; consider it their benefactor in a hundred ways, and observe its changes for a hundred purposes."

Another myth regarding cremation is given by Adam Johnston, in Schoolcraft [1] and relates to the Bonaks, or root-diggers:

"The first Indians that lived were coyotes. When one of their number died the body became full of little animals or spirits, as they thought them. After crawling over the body for a time they took all manner of shapes, some that of the deer, others the elk, antelope, etc. It was discovered, however, that great numbers were taking wings, and for a while they sailed about in the air, but eventually they would fly off to the moon. The old coyotes or Indians, fearing the earth might become depopulated in this way, concluded to stop it at once, and ordered that when one of their people died the body must be burnt. Ever after they continued to burn the bodies of deceased persons."

Ross Cox [2] gives an account of the process as performed by the Tolkotins of Oregon:

"The ceremonies attending the dead are very singular, and quite peculiar to this tribe. The body of the deceased is kept nine days laid out in his lodge, and on the tenth it is buried. For this purpose a rising ground is selected, on which are laid a number of sticks, about seven feet long, of cypress, neatly split, and in the interstices is placed a quantity of gummy wood. During these operations invitations are dispatched to the natives of the neighboring villages requesting their attendance at the ceremony. When the preparations are perfected the corpse is placed on the pile, which is

---

[1] Hist. Indian tribes of the United Stales, 1854, part IV, p. 224
[2] Adventures on the Columbia River, 1831, vol. ii, p. 387

immediately ignited, and during the process of burning, the bystanders appear to be in a high state of merriment. If a stranger happen to be present they invariably plunder him, but if that pleasure be denied them, they never separate without quarreling among themselves. Whatever property the deceased possessed is placed about the corpse, and if he happened to be a person of consequence, his friends generally purchase a capote, a shirt, a pair of trousers, etc., which articles are also laid around the pile. If the doctor who attended him has escaped uninjured, he is obliged to be present at the ceremony, and for the last time tries his skill in restoring the defunct to animation. Failing in this, he throws on the body a piece of leather, or some other article, as a present, which in some measure appeases the resentment of his relatives, and preserves the unfortunate quack from being maltreated. During the nine days the corpse is laid out the widow of the deceased is obliged to sleep along side it from sunset to sunrise; and from this custom there is no relaxation even during the hottest days of summer! While the doctor is performing his last operations she must lie on the pile, and after the fire is applied to it she cannot stir until the doctor orders her to be removed, which, however, is never done until her body is completely covered with blisters. After being placed on her legs, she is obliged to pass her hands gently through the flame and collect some of the liquid fat which issues from the corpse, with which she is permitted to wet her face and body! When the friends of the deceased observe the sinews of the legs and arms beginning to contract they compel the unfortunate widow to go again on the pile, and by dint of hard pressing to straighten those members.

"If during her husband's lifetime she has been known to have committed any act of infidelity or omitted administering to him savory food or neglected his clothing, etc, she is now made to suffer severely for such lapses of duty by his relations, who frequently fling her in the funeral pile, from which she is dragged by her friends; and thus between alternate scorching and cooling she is dragged backwards and forwards until she falls into a state of insensibility.

"After the process of burning the corpse has terminated, the widow collects the larger bones, which she rolls up in an envelope of birch bark, and which she is obliged for some years afterwards to carry on her back. She is now considered and treated as a slave, all the laborious duties of cooking, collecting fuel, etc., devolve on her. She must obey the orders of all the women, and even of the children belonging to the village, and the slightest mistake or disobedience subjects her to the infliction of a heavy punishment. The ashes of her husband are carefully collected and deposited in a grave, which it is her duty to keep free from weeds; and should any such appear, she is obliged to root them out with her fingers. During this operation her husband's relatives stand by and beat her in a cruel manner until the task is completed or she falls a victim to their brutality. The wretched widows, to avoid this complicated cruelty, frequently commit suicide. Should she, however, linger on for three or four years, the friends of her husband agree to relieve her from her painful mourning. This is a ceremony of much consequence, and the preparations for it occupy a considerable time, generally from six to eight months. The hunters proceed to the various districts in which deer and beaver abound, and after collecting large quantities of meat and fur return to the village. The skins are immediately bartered for guns, ammunition, clothing, trinkets, etc. Invitations are then bent to the inhabitants of the various friendly villages, and when they have all assembled the feast commences, and presents are distributed to each visitor. The object of their meeting is then explained, and the woman is brought forward, still carrying on her back the bones of her late husband, which are now removed and placed in a covered box, which is nailed or otherwise fastened to a post twelve feet high. Her conduct as a faithful widow is next highly eulogized, and the ceremony of her manumission is completed by one man powdering on her head the down of birds and another pouring on it the contents of a bladder of oil. She is then at liberty to marry again or lead a life of single blessedness; but few of them, I believe, wish to encounter the risk attending a second widowhood.

"The men are condemned to a similar ordeal, but they do not bear it with equal fortitude, and numbers fly to distant quarters to avoid the brutal treatment which custom has established as a kind of religious rite."

Perhaps a short review of some of the peculiar and salient points of this narrative may be permitted. It is stated that the corpse is kept nine days after death--certainly a long period of time, when it is remembered that Indians as a rule endeavor to dispose of their dead as soon as possible. This may be accounted for on the supposition that it is to give the friends and relatives an opportunity of assembling, verifying the death, and of making proper preparations for the ceremony. With regard to the verification of the dead person, William Sheldon [1] gives an account of a similar custom which was common among the Caraibs of Jamaica, and which seems to throw some light upon the unusual retention of deceased persons by the tribe in question, although it must be admitted that this is mere hypothesis:

"They had some very extraordinary customs respecting deceased persons. When one of them died, it was necessary that all his relations should see him and examine the body in order to ascertain that he died a natural death. They acted so rigidly on this principle, that if one relative remained who had not seen the body all the others could not convince that one that the death was natural. In such a case the absent relative considered himself as bound in honor to consider all the other relatives as having been accessories to the death of the kinsman, and did not rest until he had killed one of them to revenge the death of the deceased. If a Caraib died in Martinico or Guadaloupe and his relations lived in St. Vincents, it was necessary to summon them to see the body, and several months sometime elapsed before it could be finally interred. When a Caraib died he was immediately painted all over with roucou, and had his mustachios and the black streaks in his face made with a black paint, which was different from that used in their lifetime. A kind of grave was then dug in the carbet where he died, about 4 feet square and 6 or 7 feet deep. The body was let down in it, when sand was thrown in, which reached to the knees, and the body was placed in it in a sitting posture, resembling that in which they crouched round the fire or the table when alive, with the elbows on the knees and the palms of the hands against the cheeks. No part of the body touched the outside of the grave, which was covered with wood and mats until all the relations had examined it. When the customary examinations and inspections were ended the hole was filled, and the bodies afterwards remained undisturbed. The hair of the deceased was kept tied behind. In this way bodies have remained several months without any symptoms of decay or producing any disagreeable smell. The roucou not only preserved them from the sun, air, and insects during their lifetime, but probably had the same effect after death. The arms of the Caraibs were placed by them when they were covered over for inspection, and they were finally buried with them."

---

[1] Trans. Am. Antiq. Soc., 1820, vol. 1, p 377

Again, we are told that during the burning the by-standers are very merry. This hilarity is similar to that shown by the Japanese at a funeral, who rejoice that the troubles and worries of the world are over for the fortunate dead. The plundering of strangers present, it may be remembered, also took place among the Indians of the Carolinas. As already mentioned on a preceding page, the cruel manner in which the widow is treated seems to be a modification of the Hindoo suttee, but if the account be true, it would appear that death might be preferable to such torments.

It is interesting to note that in Corsica, as late as 1743, if a husband died women threw themselves upon the widow and beat her severely. Bruhier quaintly remarks that this custom obliged women to take good care of their husbands.

George Gibbs, in Schoolcraft,[1] states that among the Indians of Clear Lake, California, "the body is consumed upon a scaffold built over a hole, into which the ashes are thrown and covered"

According to Stephen Powers, [2]cremation was common among the Se-nel of California. He thus relates it--

"The dead are mostly burned. Mr. Willard described to me a scene of incremation that be once witnessed which was frightful for its exhibitions of fanatic frenzy and infatuation. The corpse was that of a wealthy chieftain, and as he lay upon the funeral pyre they placed in his mouth two gold twenties, and other smaller coins in his ears and hands, on his breast, etc., besides all his finery, his feather mantles, plumes, clothing, shell money, his fancy bows, painted arrows, etc. When the torch was applied they set up a mournful ululation, chanting and dancing about him, gradually working themselves into a wild and ecstatic raving, which seemed almost a demoniacal possession, leaping, howling, lacerating their flesh. Many seemed to lose all self-control. The younger English-speaking Indians generally lend themselves charily to such superstitious work, especially if American spectators are present, but even they were carried away by the old contagious frenzy of their race. One stripped off a broadcloth coat, quite new and fine, and ran frantically yelling and cast it upon the blazing-pile. Another rushed up and was about to throw on a pile of California

---

[1] Hist. Indian Tribes of the United States, 1853, part iii, p. 112.
[2] Contrib. to N. A. Ethnol., 1877, vol. iii, p. 169.

blankets, when a white man, to test his sincerity, offered him $16 for them, jingling the bright coins before his eyes, but the savage (for such he had become again for the moment), otherwise so avaricious, hurled him away with a yell of execration and ran and threw his offering into the flames. Squaws, even more frenzied, wildly flung upon the pyre all they had in the world--their dearest ornaments, their gaudiest dresses, their strings of glittering shells. Screaming, wailing, tearing their hair, beating their breasts in their mad and insensate infatuation, some of them would have cast themselves bodily into the flaming ruins and perished with the chief had they not been restrained by their companions. Then the bright, swift flames with their hot tongues licked this 'cold obstruction' into chemic change, and the once 'delighted spirit' of the savage was borne up....

"It seems as if the savage shared in Shakspeare's shudder at the thought of rotting in the dismal grave, for it is the one passion of his superstition to think of the soul of his departed friend set free and purified by the swift purging heat of the flames, not dragged down to be clogged and bound in the moldering body, but borne up in the soft, warm chariots of the smoke toward the beautiful sun, to bask in his warmth and light, and then, to fly away to the Happy Western Land. What wonder if the Indian shrinks with unspeakable horror from the thought of burying his friend's soul!--of pressing and ramming down with pitiless clods that inner something which once took such delight in the sweet light of the sun! What wonder if it takes years to persuade him to do otherwise and follow our custom! What wonder if even then he does it with sad fears and misgivings! Why not let him keep his custom! In the gorgeous landscapes and balmy climate of California and India incremation is as natural to the savage as it is for him to love the beauty of the sun. Let the vile Esquimaux and the frozen Siberian bury their dead if they will; it matters little, the earth is the same above as below, or to them the bosom of the earth may seem even the better; but in California do not blame the savage if he recoils at the thought of going under ground! This soft, pale halo of the lilac hills--ah, let him console himself if he will with the belief that his lost friend enjoys it still! The narrator concluded by saying that they destroyed full $500 worth of property. 'The blankets,' said he with a fine Californian scorn of such absurd insensibility to a good bargain, 'the blankets that the American offered him $16 for were not worth half the money.'

"After death the Se-nel hold that bad Indians return into coyotes. Others fall off a bridge which all souls must traverse, or are hooked off by a raging bull at the further end, while the good escape across. Like the Yokaia and the Konkan, they believe it necessary to nourish the spirits of the departed for the space of a year. This is generally done by a squaw, who takes pinole in her blanket, repairs to the scene of the incremation, or to places hallowed by the memory of the dead, where she scatters it over the ground, meantime rocking her body violently to and fro in a dance and chanting the following chorus:

> Hel-lel-li-ly,
> Hel-lel-lo,
> Hel-lel-lu.

"This refrain is repeated over and over indefinitely, but the words have no meaning whatever."

Mr. Henry Gillman [1] has published an interesting account of the exploration of a mound near Waldo, Fla., in which he found abundant evidence that cremation had existed among the former Indian population. It is as follows:

"In opening a burial-mound at Cade's Pond, a small body of water situated about two miles northeastward of Santa Fe Lake, Florida, the writer found two instances of cremation, in each of which the skull of the subject, which was unconsumed, was used as the depository of his ashes. The mound contained besides a large number of human burials, the bones being much decayed. With them were deposited a great number of vessels of pottery, many of which are painted in brilliant colors, chiefly red, yellow, and brown, and some of them ornamented with indented patterns, displaying not a little skill in the ceramic art, though they are reduced to fragments. The first of the skulls referred to was exhumed at a depth of 2 1/2 feet. It rested on its apex (base uppermost), and was filled with fragments of half incinerated human bones, mingled with dark-colored dust, and the sand which invariably sifts into crania under such circumstances. Immediately beneath the skull lay the greater part of a human tibia, presenting the peculiar compression known as a platycnemism to the degree of affording a latitudinal index of .512; while beneath and surrounding it lay the fragments of a large number of human bones, probably constituting an entire individual. In the second instance of this peculiar mode in cremation, the cranium was discovered on nearly the opposite side of the mound, at a

---

[1] Amer. Natural, November, 1878, p. 753

depth of 2 feet, and, like the former, resting on its apex. It was filled with a black mass--the residuum of burnt human bones mingled with sand. At three feet to the eastward lay the shaft of a flattened tibia, which presents the longitudinal index of .527. Both the skulls were free from all action of fire, and though subsequently crumbling to pieces on their removal, the writer had opportunity to observe their strong resemblance to the small orthocephalic crania which he had exhumed from mounds in Michigan. The same resemblance was perceptible in the other crania belonging to this mound. The small, narrow, retreating frontal, prominent parietal protuberances, rather protuberant occipital, which was not in the least compressed, the well-defined supraciliary ridges, and the superior border of the orbits, presenting a quadrilateral outline, were also particularly noticed. The lower facial bones, including the maxillaries, were wanting. On consulting such works as are accessible to him, the writer finds no mention of any similar relics having been discovered in mounds in Florida or elsewhere. For further particulars reference may be had to a paper on the subject read before the Saint Louis meeting of the American Association, August, 1878."

The discoveries made by Mr. Gillman would seem to indicate that the people whose bones he excavated resorted to a process of partial cremation, some examples of which will be given on another page. The use of crania as receptacles is certainly remarkable, if not unique.

The fact is well known to archaeologists that whenever cremation was practiced by Indians it was customary as a rule to throw into the blazing pyre all sorts of articles supposed to be useful to the dead, but no instance is known of such a wholesale destruction of property as occurred when the Indians of southern Utah burned their dead, for Dr. E. Foreman relates, in the American Naturalist for July, 1876, the account of the exploration of a mound in that Territory, which proved that at the death of a person not only were the remains destroyed by fire, but all articles of personal property, even the very habitation which had served as a home. After the process was completed, what remained unburned was covered with earth and a mound formed.

A. S. Tiffany [1] describes what he calls a cremation-furnace, discovered within seven miles of Davenport, Iowa:

---

[1] Proc. Dav. Acad. Nat Soc., 1867-76, p. 64.

"... Mound seven miles below the city, a projecting point known as Eagle Point. The surface was of the usual black soil to the depth of from 6 to 8 inches. Next was found a burnt indurated clay, resembling in color and texture a medium-burned brick, and about 30 inches in depth. Immediately beneath this clay was a bed of charred human remains 6 to 18 inches thick. This rested upon the unchanged and undisturbed loess of the bluffs, which formed the floor of the pit. Imbedded in this floor of unburned clay were a few very much decomposed, but unburned, human bones. No implements of any kind were discovered The furnace appears to have been constructed by excavating the pit and placing at the bottom of it the bodies or skeletons which had possibly been collected from scaffolds, and placing the fuel among and above the bodies, with a covering of poles or split timbers extending over and resting upon the earth, with the clay covering above, which latter we now find resting upon the charred remains. The ends of the timber covering, where they were protected by the earth above and below, were reduced to charcoal, parallel pieces of which were found at right angles to the length of the mound. No charcoal was found among or near the remains, the combustion there having been complete. The porous and softer portions of the bones were reduced to pulverized bone-black. Mr. Stevens also examined the furnace. The mound had probably not been opened after the burning."

This account is doubtless true, but the inferences may be incorrect. Many more accounts of cremation among different tribes might be given to show how prevalent was the custom, but the above are thought to be sufficiently distinctive to serve as examples.

PARTIAL CREMATION

ALLIED somewhat to cremation is a peculiar mode of burial which is supposed to have taken place among the Cherokees or some other tribe of North Carolina, and which is thus described by J. W Foster. [1]

"Up to 1819 the Cherokees held possession of this region, when, in pursuance of a treaty, they vacated a portion of the lands lying in the valley of the Little Tennessee River. In 1821 Mr. McDowell commenced farming. During the first season's operations the plowshare, in passing over a certain portion of a field, produced a hollow rumbling sound, and in exploring for the cause the first object met with was a shallow layer of charcoal, beneath which was a slab of burnt clay about 7 feet in length and 4 feet broad, which, in the attempt to remove, broke into several fragments. Nothing beneath this slab was found, but on examining its under side, to his great surprise there was the mould of a naked human figure. Three of these burned clay sepulchers were thus raised and examined during the first year of his occupancy, since which time none have been found until recently…. During the past season (1872) the plow brought up another fragment of one of these moulds, revealing the impress of a plump human arm.

"Col. C. W. Jenkes, the superintendent of the Corundum mines, which have recently been opened in that vicinity, advises me thus:

"'We have Indians all about us, with traditions extending back for 500 years. In this time they have buried their dead under huge piles of stones. We have at one point the remains of 600 warriors under one pile, but a grave has just been opened of the following construction: A pit was dug, into which the corpse was placed, face upward; then over it was moulded a covering of mortar, fitting the form and features. On this was built a hot fire, which formed an entire shield of pottery for the corpse. The breaking up of one such tomb gives a perfect cast of the form of the occupant.'

"Colonel Jenkes, fully impressed with the value of these archaeological discoveries, detailed a man to superintend the exhumation, who pro-

---

[1] Pre-Historic Races, 1873, p. 149.

ceeded to remove the earth from the mould, which he reached through a layer of charcoal, and then with a trowel excavated beneath it. The clay was not thoroughly baked, and no impression of the corpse was left, except of the forehead and that portion of the limbs between the ankles and the knees, and even these portions of the mould crumbled. The body had been placed east and west, the head toward the east. 'I had hoped,' continues Mr. McDowell, 'that the cast in the clay would be as perfect as one I found 51 years ago, a fragment of which I presented to Colonel Jenkes, with the impression of a part of the arm on one side and on the other of the fingers, that had pressed down the soft clay upon the body interred beneath.' The mound-builders of the Ohio Valley, as has been shown, often placed a layer of clay over the dead, but not in immediate contact, upon which they builded fires; and the evidence that cremation was often resorted to in their disposition are too abundant to be gainsaid."

This statement is corroborated by Mr. Wilcox: [1]

"Mr. Wilcox also stated that when recently in North Carolina his attention was called to an unusual method of burial by an ancient race of Indians in that vicinity. In numerous instances burial places were discovered where the bodies had been placed with the face up and covered with a coating of plastic clay about an inch thick. A pile of wood was then placed on top and fired, which consumed the body and baked the clay, which retained the impression of the body. This was then lightly covered with earth."

It is thought no doubt can attach to the statements given, but the cases are remarkable as being the only instances of the kind met with in the extensive range of reading preparatory to a study of the subject of burial, although it must be observed that Bruhier states that the ancient Ethiopians covered the corpses of their dead with plaster (probably mud), but they did not burn these curious coffins.

Another method, embracing both burial and cremation, has been practiced by the Pitt River or Achomawi Indians of California, who "bury the body in the ground in a standing position, the shoulders nearly even with the ground. The grave is prepared by digging a hole of sufficient depth and circumference to admit the body, the head being cut off. In the grave are placed the bows and arrows, bead-work, trappings, &c., belonging to the

---

[1] Proc. Acad. Nat. Soc. Phila., Nov 1874, p 168.

deceased; quantities of food, consisting of dried fish, roots, herbs, &c., were placed with the body also. The grave was then filled up, covering the headless body; then a bundle of fagots was brought and placed on the grave by the different members of the tribe, and on these fagots the head was placed, the pile fired, and the head consumed to ashes; after this was done, the female relatives of the deceased, who had appeared as mourners with their faces blackened with a preparation resembling tar or paint, dipped their fingers in the ashes of the cremated head and made three marks on their right cheek. This constituted the mourning garb, the period of which lasted until this black substance wore off from the face. In addition to this mourning, the blood female relatives of the deceased (who, by the way, appeared to be a man of distinction) had their hair cropped short. I noticed while the head was burning that the old women of the tribe sat on the ground, forming a large circle, inside of which another circle of young girls were formed standing and swaying their bodies to and fro and singing a mournful ditty. This was the only burial of a male that I witnessed. The custom of burying females is very different, their bodies being wrapped or bundled up in skins and laid away in caves, with their valuables, and in some cases food being placed with them in their mouths. Occasionally money is left to pay for food in the spirit land."

This account is furnished by General Charles H. Tompkins, deputy quartermaster-general, United States Army, who witnessed the burial above related, and is the more interesting as it seems to be the only well-authenticated case on record, although E. A. Barber [1] has described what may possibly have been a case of cremation like the one above noted:

"A very singular case of aboriginal burial was brought to my notice recently by Mr. William Klingbeil, of Philadelphia. On the New Jersey bank of the Delaware River, a short distance below Gloucester City, the skeleton of a man was found buried in a standing position, in a high, red, sandy-clay bluff overlooking the stream. A few inches below the surface the neck bones were found, and below these the remainder of the skeleton, with the exception of the bones of the hands and feet. The skull being wanting, it could not be determined whether the remains were those of an Indian or of a white man, but in either case the sepulture was peculiarly aboriginal. A careful exhumation and critical examination by Mr. Klingbeil disclosed the fact that around the lower extremities of the body had been placed a

---

[1] American Natural, Sept., 1878, p. 699.

number of large stones, which revealed traces of fire, in conjunction with charred wood, and the bones of the feet had undoubtedly been consumed. This fact makes it appear reasonably certain that the subject had been executed, probably as a prisoner of war. A pit had been dug, in which he was placed erect, and a fire kindled around him. Then he had been buried alive, or, at least, if he did not survive the fiery ordeal, his body was imbedded in the earth, with the exception of his head, which was left protruding above the surface. As no trace of the cranium could be found, it seems probable that the head had either been burned or severed from the body and removed, or else left a prey to ravenous birds. The skeleton, which would have measured fully six feet in height, was undoubtedly that of a man."

Blacking the face, as is mentioned in the first account, is a custom known to have existed among many tribes throughout the world, but in some cases different earths and pigments are used as signs of mourning. The natives of Guinea smear a chalky substance over their bodies as an outward expression of grief, and it is well known that the ancient Israelites threw ashes on their heads and garments. Placing food with the corpse or in its mouth, and money in the hand, finds its analogue in the custom of the ancient Romans, who, some time before interment, placed a piece of money in the corpse's mouth, which was thought to be Charon's fare for wafting the departed soul over the Infernal River. Besides this, the corpse's mouth was furnished with a certain cake, composed of flour, honey, &c. This was designed to appease the fury of Cerberus, the infernal doorkeeper, and to procure a safe and quiet entrance. These examples are curious coincidences, if nothing more.

BURIAL ABOVE GROUND

OUR attention should next be turned to sepulture above the ground, including lodge, house, box, scaffold, tree, and canoe burial, and the first example which may be given is that of burial in lodges, which is by no means common. The description which follows is by Stansbury,[1] and relates to the Sioux:

"I put on my moccasins, and, displaying my wet shirt like a flag to the wind, we proceeded to the lodges which had attracted our curiosity. There were five of them pitched upon the open prairie, and in them we found the bodies of nine Sioux laid out upon the ground, wrapped in their robes of buffalo-skin, with their saddles, spears, camp-kettles, and all their accoutrements piled up around them. Some lodges contained three, others only one body, all of which were more or less in a state of decomposition. A short distance apart from these was one lodge which, though small, seemed of rather superior pretensions, and was evidently pitched with great care. It contained the body of a young Indian girl of sixteen or eighteen years, with a countenance presenting quite an agreeable expression; she was richly dressed in leggins of fine scarlet cloth elaborately ornamented; a new pair of moccasins, beautifully embroidered with porcupine quills, was on her feet, and her body was wrapped in two superb buffalo-robes worked in like manner; she had evidently been dead but a day or two, and to our surprise a portion of the upper part of her person was bare, exposing the face and a part of the breast, as if the robes in which she was wrapped had by some means been disarranged, whereas all the other bodies were closely covered up. It was, at the time, the opinion of our mountaineers that these Indians must have fallen in an encounter with a party of Crows; but I subsequently learned that they had all died of the cholera, and that this young girl, being considered past recovery, had been arranged by her friends in the habiliments of the dead, inclosed in the lodge alive, and abandoned to her fate, so fearfully alarmed were the Indians by this to them novel and terrible disease."

---

[1] Explorations of the Valley of the Great Salt Lake of Utah, 1852, p. 43.

It might, perhaps, be said that this form of burial was exceptional, and due to the dread of again using the lodges which had served as the homes of those afflicted with the cholera, but it is thought such was not the case, as the writer has notes of the same kind of burial among the same tribe and of others, notably the Crows, the body of one of their chiefs (Long Horse) being disposed of as follows.

"The lodge poles inclose an oblong circle some 18 by 22 feet at the base, converging to a point at least 30 feet high, covered with buffalo-hides dressed without hair except a part of the tail switch, which floats outside like, and mingled with human scalps. The different skins are neatly fitted and sewed together with sinew, and all painted in seven alternate horizontal stripes of brown and yellow, decorated with various life-like war scenes. Over the small entrance is a large bright cross, the upright being a large stuffed white wolf- skin upon his war lance, and the cross-bar of bright scarlet flannel, containing the quiver of bow and arrows, which nearly all warriors still carry, even when armed with repeating rifles. As the cross is not a pagan but a Christian (which Long Horse was not either by profession or practice) emblem, it was probably placed there by the influence of some of his white friends. I entered, finding Long Horse buried Indian fashion, in full-war dress, paint and feathers, in a rude coffin, upon a platform about breast high, decorated with weapons, scalps, and ornaments. A large opening and wind-flap at top favored ventilation, and though he had lain there in an open coffin a full month, some of which was hot weather, there was but little effluvia; in fact, I have seldom found much in a burial-teepee, and when this mode of burial is thus performed it is less repulsive than natural to suppose."

This account is furnished by Col. P. W. Norris, superintendent of Yellowstone National Park, he having been an eye-witness of what he relates in 1876.

The Blackfeet, Sioux, and Navajos also bury in lodges, and the Indians of Bellingham Bay, according to Dr. J. F. Hammond, U. S. A., place their dead in carved wooden sarcophagi, inclosing these with a rectangular tent of some white material.

Bancroft [1] states that certain of the Indians of Costa Rica, when a death occurred, deposited the body in a small hut constructed of plaited palm reeds. In this it is preserved for three years, food being supplied, and on each anniversary of the death it is redressed and attended to amid certain ceremonies. The writer has been recently informed that a similar custom prevailed in Demerara. No authentic accounts are known of analogous modes of burial among the peoples of the Old World, although quite frequently the dead were interred beneath the floors of their houses, a custom which has been followed by the Mosquito Indians of Central America and one or two of our own tribes.

---

[1] Nat. Races of Pac. States, 1874, vol. 1, p. 780.

BOX BURIAL

UNDER this head may be placed those examples furnished by certain tribes on the Northwest coast who used as receptacles for the dead wonderfully carved, large wooden chests, these being supported upon a low platform or resting on the ground. In shape they resemble a small house with an angular roof, and each one has an opening through which food may be passed to the corpse.

Some of the tribes formerly living in New York used boxes much resembling those spoken of, and the Creeks, Choctaws, and Cherokees did the same.

Capt J. H. Gageby, U. S. A., furnishes the following relating to the Creeks in Indian Territory:

"... are buried on the surface, in a box or a substitute made of branches of trees, covered with small branches, leaves, and earth. I have seen several of their graves, which after a few weeks had become uncovered and the remains exposed to view. I saw in one Creek grave (a child's) a small sum of silver, in another (adult male) some implements of warfare, bow and arrows. They are all interred with the feet of the corpse to the east. In the mourning ceremonies of the Creeks the nearer relatives smeared their hair and faces with a composition made of grease and wood ashes, and would remain in that condition for several days, and probably a month."

TREE AND SCAFFOLD BURIAL

WE may now pass to what may be called aerial sepulture proper, the most common examples of which are tree and scaffold burial, quite extensively practiced even at the present time. From what can be learned, the choice of this mode depends greatly on the facilities present; where timber abounds, trees being used; if absent, scaffolds being employed, the construction of which among the Yanktonais is related as follows: [1]

"These scaffolds are 7 to 8 feet high, 10 feet long, and 4 or 5 wide. Four stout posts, with forked ends, are first set firmly in the ground, and then in the forks are laid cross and side poles, on which is made a flooring of small poles. The body is then carefully wrapped, so as to make it watertight, and laid to rest on the poles. The reason why Indians bury in the open air instead of under the ground is for the purpose of protecting their dead from wild animals. In new countries, where wolves and bears are numerous, a dead body will be dug up and devoured, though it be put many feet under the ground. I noticed many little buckets and baskets hanging on the scaffolds.... These had contained food and drink for the dead. I asked Washtella if she was sure the soul ate and drank on its journey, and if the food did not remain untouched in its basket. She replied, 'Oh, no, the food and water is always gone.' I looked at the hundreds of ravens perched on the scaffolds and could account for what became of most of the food and water."...

John Young, Indian agent at the Blackfeet Agency, Montana, sends the following account of tree-burial among this tribe:

"Their manner of burial has always been (until recently) to inclose the dead body in robes or blankets, the best owned by the departed, closely sewed up, and then, if a male or chief, fasten in the branches of a tree so high as to be beyond the reach of wolves, and then left to slowly waste in the dry winds. If the body was that of a squaw or child, it was thrown into the underbrush or jungle, where it soon became the prey of the wild animals.

---

[1] Life of Belden, the White Chief, 1871, p. 87.

The weapons, pipes, &c., of men were inclosed, and the small toys of children with them. The ceremonies were equally barbarous, the relatives cutting off, according to the depth of their grief, one or more joints of the fingers, divesting themselves of clothing even in the coldest weather, and filling the air with their lamentations. All the sewing up and burial process was conducted by the squaws, as the men would not touch nor remain in proximity to a dead body.

"When an Indian of any importance is departing, the squaws assemble in the lodge or teepee and sing the death-song, recounting the prowess and virtues of the dying one, and the oldest man at hand goes into the open air and solemnly addresses the 'Great Spirit,' bespeaking a welcome for him into the happy hunting grounds. Whatever property the deceased has-- lodge, arms, or ponies--if a will was made, it was carefully carried out; if not, all was scrambled for by the relatives. I have often had, when a man wanted to go out of mourning, to supply the necessary clothing to cover his nakedness.

"Further mourning observances were and are, the women relatives getting on some elevated spot near where the body rests, and keeping up a dismal wail, frequently even in extreme cold weather, the greater part of the night, and this is kept up often for a month. No cremation or burying in a grave was practiced by them at any time. Pained by often coming on skeletons in trees and the stench of half-consumed remains in the brush, and shocked by the frequent mutilations visible, I have reasoned with the poor savages. In one case, when a woman was about to cut off a finger in evidence of her grief for the loss of a child, she consented on entreaty to cut off only one joint, and on further entreaty was brought to merely making a cut and letting out some blood. This much she could not be prevailed upon to forego.... Their mourning and wailing, avoiding the defilement of touching a dead body, and other customs not connected with burial observances, strongly point to Jewish origin."

Keating [1] thus describes burial scaffolds:

"On these scaffolds, which are from 8 to 10 feet high, corpses were deposited in a box made from part of a broken canoe. Some hair was suspended, which we at first mistook for a scalp, but our guide informed us

---

[1] Long's Exped. to the St. Peter's River, 1834, p. 392.

that these were locks of hair torn from their heads by the relatives to testify their grief. In the centre, between the four posts which supported the scaffold, a stake was planted in the ground; it was about six feet high, and bore an imitation of human figures, five of which had a design of a petticoat, indicating them to be females; the rest, amounting to seven, were naked, and were intended for male figures; of the latter four were headless, showing that they had been slain; the three other male figures were unmutilated, but held a staff in their hand, which, as our guide informed us, designated that they were slaves. The post, which is an usual accompaniment to the scaffold that supports a warrior's remains, does not represent the achievements of the deceased; but those of the warriors that assembled near his remains danced the dance of the post, and related their martial exploits. A number of small bones of animals were observed in the vicinity, which were probably left there after a feast celebrated in honor of the dead.

"The boxes in which the corpses were placed are so short that a man could not lie in them extended at full length, but in a country where boxes and boards are scarce this is overlooked. After the corpses have remained a certain time exposed, they are taken down and buried. Our guide, Renville, related to us that he had been a witness to an interesting, though painful, circumstance that occurred here. An Indian who resided on the Mississippi, hearing that his son had died at this spot, came up in a canoe to take charge of the remains and convey them down the river to his place of abode, but on his arrival he found that the corpse had already made such progress toward decomposition as rendered it impossible for it to be removed. He then undertook, with a few friends, to clean off the bones. All the flesh was scraped off and thrown into the stream, the bones were carefully collected into his canoe, and subsequently carried down to his residence."

Interesting and valuable from the extreme attention paid to details is the following account of a burial case discovered by Dr. George M. Sternberg, U. S. A., and furnished by Dr. George A. Otis, U. S. A., Army Medical Museum, Washington, D.C. It relates to the Cheyennes of Kansas:

"The case was found, Brevet Major Sternberg states, on the banks of Walnut Creek, Kansas, elevated about eight feet from the ground by four notched poles, which were firmly planted in the ground. The unusual care manifested in the preparation of the case induced Dr. Sternberg to infer that some important chief was inclosed in it. Believing that articles of interest were inclosed with the body, and that their value would be enhanced if they were received at the Museum as left by the Indians, Dr. Sternberg determined to send the case unopened.

"I had the case opened this morning and an inventory made of the contents. The case consisted of a cradle of interlaced branches of white willow, about 6 feet long, 3 feet broad, and 3 feet high, with a flooring of buffalo thongs arranged as a net-work. This cradle was securely fastened by strips of buffalo-hide to four poles of ironwood and cottonwood, about 12 feet in length. These poles doubtless rested upon the forked extremities of the vertical poles described by Dr. Sternberg. The cradle was wrapped in two buffalo-robes of large size and well preserved. On removing these an aperture 18 inches square was found at the middle of the right side of the cradle or basket. Within appeared other buffalo-robes folded about the remains, and secured by gaudy-colored sashes. Five robes were successively removed, making seven in all. Then we came to a series of new blankets folded about the remains. There were five in all--two scarlet, two blue, and one white. These being removed, the next wrappings consisted of a striped white and gray sack, and of a United States Infantry overcoat, like the other coverings nearly new. We had now come apparently upon the immediate envelopes of the remains, which it was now evident must be those of a child. These consisted of three robes, with hoods very richly ornamented with bead-work. These robes or cloaks were of buffalo-calf skin about four feet in length, elaborately decorated with bead-work in stripes. The outer was covered with rows of blue and white bead-work, the second was green and yellow, and the third blue and red. All were further adorned by spherical brass bells attached all about the borders by strings of beads.

"The remains with their wrappings lay upon a matting similar to that used by the Navajo and other Indians of the southern plains, and upon a pillow of dirty rags, in which were folded a bag of red paint, bits of antelope skin, bunches of straps, buckles, &c. The three bead-work hooded cloaks were now removed, and then we successively unwrapped a gray woolen double shawl, five yards of blue cassimere, six yards of red calico, and six yards of brown calico, and finally disclosed the remains of a child, probably about a year old, in an advanced stage of decomposition. The cadaver had a beaver-cap ornamented with disks of copper containing the bones of the cranium, which had fallen apart. About the neck were long wampum necklaces with dentalium, unionida, and auricula, interspersed with beads.

There were also strings of the pieces of Haliotis from the Gulf of California, so valued by the Indians on this side of the Rocky Mountains. The body had been elaborately dressed for burial, the costume consisting of a red- flannel cloak, a red tunic, and frock-leggins adorned with bead-work, yarn stockings of red and black worsted, and deerskin bead-work moccasins. With the remains were numerous trinkets, a porcelain image, a China vase, strings of beads, several toys, a pair of mittens, a fur collar, a pouch of the skin of putorius vison, &c."

Another extremely interesting account of scaffold burial, furnished by Dr. L. S. Turner, U. S. A., Fort Peck, Mont., and relating to the Sioux, is here given entire, as it refers to certain curious mourning observances which have prevailed to a great extent over the entire globe:

"The Dakotas bury their dead in the tops of trees when limbs can be found sufficiently horizontal to support scaffolding on which to lay the body, but as such growth is not common in Dakota, the more general practice is to lay them upon scaffolds from 7 to 10 feet high and out of the reach of carnivorous animals as the wolf. These scaffolds are constructed upon four posts set into the ground something after the manner of the rude drawing which I inclose. Like all labors of a domestic kind, the preparation for burial is left to the women, usually the old women. The work begins as soon as life is extinct. The face, neck, and hands are thickly painted with vermilion, or a species of red earth found in various portions of the Territory when the vermilion of the traders cannot be had. The clothes and personal trinkets of the deceased ornament the body. When blankets are available, it is then wrapped in one, all parts of the body being completely enveloped. Around this a dressed skin of buffalo is then securely wrapped, with the flesh side out, and the whole securely bound with thongs of skins, either raw or dressed; and for ornament, when available, a bright-red blanket envelopes all other coverings, and renders the general scene more picturesque until dimmed by time and the elements. As soon as the scaffold is ready, the body is borne by the women, followed by the female relatives, to the place of final deposit, and left prone in its secure wrappings upon this airy bed of death. This ceremony is accompanied with lamentations so wild and weird that one must see and hear in order to appreciate. If the deceased be a brave, it is customary to place upon or beneath the scaffold a few buffalo-heads which time has rendered dry and inoffensive; and if he has been brave in war some of his implements of battle are placed on the scaffold or securely tied to its timbers. If the deceased has been a chief, or a soldier related to his chief, it is not uncommon to slay his favorite pony and place the body beneath the scaffold, under the superstition, I suppose, that the horse goes with the man. As illustrating the propensity to provide the dead with the things used while living, I may mention that some years ago I loaned to an old man a delft urinal for the use of his son, a young man who was slowly dying of a wasting disease. I made him promise faithfully that he would return it as soon as his son was done using it. Not long afterwards the urinal graced the scaffold which held the remains of the dead warrior, and as it has not to this day been returned I presume the young man is not done using it.

"The mourning customs of the Dakotas, though few of them appear to be of universal observance, cover considerable ground. The hair, never cut under other circumstances, is cropped off even with the neck, and the top of the head and forehead, and sometimes nearly the whole body, are smeared with a species of white earth resembling chalk, moistened with water. The lodge, teepee, and all the family possessions except the few shabby articles of apparel worn by the mourners, are given away and the family left destitute. Thus far the custom is universal or nearly so. The wives, mother, and sisters of a deceased man, on the first, second, or third day after the funeral, frequently throw off their moccasins and leggins and gash their legs with their butcher- knives, and march through the camp and to the place of burial with bare and bleeding extremities, while they chant or wail their dismal songs of mourning. The men likewise often gash themselves in many places, and usually seek the solitude of the higher point on the distant prairie, where they remain fasting, smoking, and wailing out their lamentations for two or three days. A chief who had lost a brother once came to me after three or four days of mourning in solitude almost exhausted from hunger and bodily anguish. He had gashed the outer side of both lower extremities at intervals of a few inches all the way from the ankles to the top of the hips. His wounds had inflamed from exposure, and were suppurating freely. He assured me that he had not slept for several days or nights. I dressed his wounds with a soothing ointment, and gave him a full dose of an effective anodyne, after which he slept long and refreshingly, and awoke to express his gratitude and shake my hand in a very cordial and sincere manner. When these harsher inflictions are not resorted to, the mourners usually repair daily for a few days to the place of burial, toward the hour of sunset, and chant their grief until apparently assuaged by its own expression. This is rarely kept up for more than four or five days, but is occasionally resorted to, at intervals, for weeks, or even months, according to the mood of the bereft. I have seen few things in life so touching as the spectacle of an old father going daily to the grave of his child, while the shadows are lengthening, and pouring out his grief in wails that would move a demon, until his figure melts with the gray twilight, when, silent and solemn, he returns to his desolate family. The weird effect of this observance is sometimes heightened, when the deceased was a grown-up son, by the old man kindling a little fire near the head of the scaffold, and varying his lamentations with smoking in silence. The foregoing is drawn from my memory of personal observances during a period of more than six years' constant intercourse with several subdivisions of the Dakota Indians. There may be much which memory has failed to recall upon a brief consideration."

Perhaps a brief review of Dr. Turner's narrative may not be deemed inappropriate here.

Supplying food to the dead is a custom which is known to be of great antiquity; in some instances, as among the ancient Romans, it appears to have been a sacrificial offering, for it usually accompanied cremation, and was not confined to food alone, for spices, perfumes, oil, etc., were thrown upon the burning pile. In addition to this, articles supposed or known to have been agreeable to the deceased were also consumed. The Jews did the same, and in our own time the Chinese, Caribe and many of the tribes of North American Indians followed these customs. The cutting of hair as a mourning observance is of very great antiquity, and Tegg relates that among the ancients whole cities and countries were shaved (sic) when a great man died. The Persians not only shaved themselves on such occasions, but extended the same process to their domestic animals, and Alexander, at the death of Hephastin, not only cut off the manes of his horses and mules, but took down the battlements from the city walls, that even towns might seem in mourning and look bald. Scarifying and mutilating the body has prevailed from a remote period of time, having possibly replaced, in the process of evolution, to a certain extent, the more barbarous practice of absolute personal sacrifice. In later days, among our Indians, human sacrifices have taken place to only a limited extent, but formerly many victims were immolated, for at the funerals of the chiefs of the Florida and Carolina Indians all the male relatives and wives were slain, for the reason, according to Gallatin, that the hereditary dignity of Chief or Great Sun descended, as usual, by the female line; and he, as well as all other members of his clan, whether male or female, could marry only persons of an inferior clan. To this day mutilation of the person among some tribes of Indians is usual. The sacrifice of the favorite horse or horses is by no means peculiar to our Indians, for it was common among the Romans, and possibly even among the men of the Reindeer period, for at Solutre, in France, the writer saw horses' bones exhumed from the graves examined in 1873. The writer has frequently conversed with Indians upon this subject, and they have invariably informed him that when horses were slain great care was taken to select the poorest of the band.

Tree-burial was not uncommon among the nations of antiquity, for the Colchiens enveloped their dead in sacks of skin and hung them to trees; the ancient Tartars and Scythians did the same. With regard to the use of scaffolds and trees as places of deposit for the dead, it seems somewhat curious that the tribes who formerly occupied the eastern portion of our continent were not in the habit of burying in this way, which, from the abundance of timber, would have been a much easier method than the ones in vogue, while the western tribes, living in sparsely wooded localities, preferred the other. If we consider that the Indians were desirous of preserving their dead as long as possible, the fact of their dead being placed in trees and scaffolds would lead to the supposition that those living on the plains were well aware of the desiccating property of the dry air of that arid region. This desiccation would pass for a kind of mummification.

The particular part of the mourning ceremonies, which consisted in loud cries and lamentations, may have had in early periods of time a greater significance than that of a mere expression of grief or woe, and on this point Bruhier [1] seems quite positive, his interpretation being that such cries were intended to prevent premature burial. He gives some interesting examples, which may be admitted here.

"The Caribs lament loudly, their wailings being interspersed with comical remarks and questions to the dead as to why he preferred to leave this world, having everything to make life comfortable. They place the corpse on a little seat in a ditch or grave four or five feet deep, and for ten days they bring food, requesting the corpse to eat. Finally, being convinced that the dead will neither eat nor return to life, they throw the food on the head of the corpse and fill up the grave."

---

[1] L' des signes de la Mort, 1742, I, p. 475 et seq.

When one died among the Romans, the nearest parents embraced the body, closed the eyes and mouth, and when one was about to die received the last words and sighs, and then loudly called the name of the dead, finally bidding an eternal adieu. This ceremony of calling the deceased by name was known as the conclamation, and was a custom anterior even to the foundation of Rome. One dying away from home was immediately removed thither, in order that this might be performed with greater propriety. In Picardy, as late as 1743, the relatives threw themselves on the corpse and with loud cries called it by name, and up to 1855 the Moravians of Pennsylvania, at the death of one of their number, performed mournful musical airs on brass instruments from the village church steeple and again at the grave [1] This custom, however, was probably a remnant of the ancient funeral observances, and not to prevent premature burial, or, perhaps, to scare away bad spirits.

W. L. Hardisty [2] gives a curious example of log-burial in trees, relating to the Loucheux of British America:

"They inclose the body in a neatly-hollowed piece of wood, and secure it to two or more trees, about six feet from the ground. A log about eight feet long is first split in two, and each of the parts carefully hollowed out to the required size. The body is then inclosed and the two pieces well lashed together, preparatory to being finally secured, as before stated, to the trees"

With regard to the use of scaffolds as places of deposit for the dead, the following theories by Dr. W. Gardner, U.S.A., are given:

"If we come to inquire why the American aborigines placed the dead bodies of their relatives and friends in trees, or upon scaffolds resembling trees, instead of burying them in the ground, or burning them and preserving their ashes in urns, I think we can answer the inquiry by recollecting that most if not all the tribes of American Indians, as well as other nations of a higher civilization, believed that the human soul, spirit or immortal part, was of the form and nature of a bird, and as these are essentially arboreal in their habits, it is quite in keeping to suppose that the

---

[1] The writer is informed by Mr. John Henry Boner that this custom still prevails not only in Pennsylvania, but at the Moravian settlement of Salem, North Carolina.
[2] Rep. Smithsonian Inst., 1866, p. 319

soul-bird would have readier access to its former home or dwelling-place if it was placed upon a tree or scaffold than if it was buried in the earth; moreover, from this lofty eyrie the souls of the dead could rest secure from the attacks of wolves or other profane beasts, and guard like sentinels the homes and hunting-grounds of their loved ones."

This statement is given because of a corroborative note in the writer's possession, but he is not prepared to admit it as correct without farther investigation.

PARTIAL SCAFFOLD BURIAL AND OSSUARIES

UNDER this heading may be placed the burials which consisted in first depositing the bodies on scaffolds, where they were allowed to remain for a variable length of time, after which the bones were cleaned and deposited either in the earth or in special structures called by writers "bone-houses." Roman [1] relates the following concerning the Choctaws:

"The following treatment of the dead is very strange ... As soon as the deceased is departed, a stage is erected (as in the annexed plate is represented) and the corpse is laid on it and covered with a bear skin; if he be a man of note, it is decorated, and the poles painted red with vermillion and bear's oil; if a child, it is put upon stakes set across; at this stage the relations come and weep, asking many questions of the corpse, such as, why he left them? did not his wife serve him well? was he not contented with his children? had he not corn enough? did not his land produce sufficient of everything? was he afraid of his enemies? etc. and this accompanied by loud howlings; the women will be there constantly, and sometimes with the corrupted air and heat of the sun faint so as to oblige the bystanders to carry them home; the men will also come and mourn in the same manner, but in the night or at other unseasonable times, when they are least likely to be discovered.

"The stage is fenced round with poles; it remains thus a certain time but not a fixed space; this is sometimes extended to three or four months, but seldom more than half that time. A certain set of venerable old Gentlemen who wear very long nails as a distinguishing badge on the thumb, fore and middle finger of each hand, constantly travel through the nation (when i was there, i was told there were but five of this respectable order) that one of them may acquaint those concerned, of the expiration of this period, which is according to their own fancy; the day being come, the friends and relations assemble near the stage, a fire is made, and the respectable operator, after the body is taken down, with his nails tears the remaining flesh off the bones, and throws it with the entrails into the fire, where it is

---

[1] Hist. of Florida, 1775, p. 89.

consumed; then he scrapes the bones and burns the scrapings likewise; the head being painted red with vermillion is with the rest of the bones put into a neatly made chest (which for a Chief is also made red) and deposited in the loft of a hut built for that purpose, and called bone house; each town has one of these; after remaining here one year or thereabouts, if he be a man of any note, they take the chest down, and in an assembly of relations and friends they weep once more over him, refresh the colour of the head, paint the box, and then deposit him to lasting oblivion.

"An enemy nor one who commits suicide is buried under the earth as one to be directly forgotten and unworthy the above ceremonial obsequies and mourning."

Jones [1] quotes one of the older writers, as follows, regarding the Natchez tribe:

"Among the Natchez the dead were either inhumed or placed in tombs. These tombs were located within or very near their temples. They rested upon four forked sticks fixed fast in the ground, and were raised some three feet above the earth. About eight feet long and a foot and a half wide, they were prepared for the reception of a single corpse. After the body was placed upon it, a basket-work of twigs was woven around and covered with mud, an opening being left at the head, through which food was presented to the deceased. When the flesh had all rotted away, the bones were taken out, placed in a box made of canes, and then deposited in the temple. The common dead were mourned and lamented for a period of three days. Those who fell in battle were honored with a more protracted and grievous lamentation."

Bartram [2] gives a somewhat different account from Roman of burial among the Choctaws of Carolina:

"The Choctaws pay their last duties and respect to the deceased in a very different manner. As soon as a person is dead, they erect a scaffold 18 or 20 feet high in a grove adjacent to the town, where they lay the corps, lightly covered with a mantle; here it is suffered to remain, visited and protected by the friends and relations, until the flesh becomes putrid, so as

---

[1] Antiquities of the Southern Indiana, 1873, p. 105.
[2] Bartram's Travel, 1791, p. 516.

easily to part from the bones; then undertakers, who make it their business, carefully strip the flesh from the bones, wash and cleanse them, and when dry and purified by the air, having provided a curiously-wrought chest or coffin, fabricated of bones and splints, they place all the bones therein, which is deposited in the bone-house, a building erected for that purpose in every town; and when this house is full a general solemn funeral takes place; when the nearest kindred or friends of the deceased, on a day appointed, repair to the bone-house, take up the respective coffins, and, following one another in order of seniority, the nearest relations and connections attending their respective corps, and the multitude following after them, all as one family, with united voice of alternate allelujah and lamentation, slowly proceeding on to the place of general interment, when they place the coffins in order, forming a pyramid; [1]and, lastly, cover all over with earth, which raises a conical hill or mount; when they return to town in order of solemn procession, concluding the day with a festival, which is called the feast of the dead."

Morgan [2] also alludes to this mode of burial:

"The body of the deceased was exposed upon a hark scaffolding erected upon poles or secured upon the limbs of trees, where it was left to waste to a skeleton. After this had been effected by the process of decomposition in the open air, the bones were removed either to the former house of the deceased, or to a small bark-house by its side, prepared for their reception. In this manner the skeletons of the whole family were preserved from generation to generation by the filial or parental affection of the living After the lapse of a number of years, or in a season of public insecurity, or on the eve of abandoning a settlement, it was customary to collect these skeletons from the whole community around and consign them to a common resting place.

"To this custom, which is not confined to the Iroquois, is doubtless to be ascribed the barrows and bone-mounds which have been found in such numbers in various parts of the country. On opening these mounds the skeletons are usually found arranged in horizontal layers, a conical

---

[1] Some ingenious men whom I have conversed with have given it as their opinion that all those pyramidal artificial hills, usually called Indian mounds, were raised on this occasion, and are generally sepulchres. However, I am of different opinion.
[2] League of the Iroquois 1851, p. 171

pyramid, those in each layer radiating from a common center. In other cases they are found placed promiscuously."

D. G. Brinton [1] likewise gives an account of the interment of collected bones:

"East of the Mississippi nearly every nation was accustomed at stated periods--usually once in eight or ten years--to collect and clean the osseous remains of those of its number who had died in the intervening time, and inter them in one common sepulcher, lined with choice furs, and marked with a mound of wood, stone, or earth. Such is the origin of those immense tumuli filled with the mortal remains of nations and generations, which the antiquary, with irreverent curiosity, so frequently chances upon in all portions of our territory. Throughout Central America the same usage obtained in various localities, as early writers and existing monuments abundantly testify. Instead of interring the bones, were they those of some distinguished chieftain, they were deposited in the temples or the council-houses, usually in small chests of canes or splints. Such were the charnel-houses which the historians of De Soto's expedition so often mention, and these are the 'arks' Adair and other authors who have sought to trace the descent of the Indians from the Jews have likened to that which the ancient Israelites bore with them in their migrations.

"A widow among the Tahkalis was obliged to carry the bones of her deceased husband wherever she went for four years, preserving them in such a casket, handsomely decorated with feathers (Rich. Arc. Exp, p. 260). The Caribs of the mainland adopted the custom for all, without exception. About a year after death the bones were cleaned, bleached, painted, wrapped in odorous balsams, placed in a wicker basket, and kept suspended from the door of their dwelling (Gumilla Hist. del Orinoco I., pp. 199, 202, 204). When the quantity of these heirlooms became burdensome they were removed to some inaccessible cavern and stowed away with reverential care."

George Catlin [2] describes what he calls the "Golgothas" of the Mandans:

---

[1] Myths of the New World, 1868. p. 256.
[2] Hist. N. A. Indians, 1844, I, p. 90.

"There are several of these golgothas, or circles of twenty or thirty feet in diameter, and in the center of each ring or circle is a little mound of three feet high, on which uniformly rest two buffalo skulls (a male and female), and in the center of the little mound is erected 'a medicine pole,' of about twenty feet high, supporting many curious articles of mystery and superstition, which they suppose have the power of guarding and protecting this sacred arrangement.

"Here, then, to this strange place do these people again resort to evince their further affections for the dead, not in groans and lamentations, however, for several years have cured the anguish, but fond affection and endearments are here renewed, and conversations are here held and cherished with the dead. Each one of these skulls is placed upon a bunch of wild sage, which has been pulled and placed under it. The wife knows, by some mark or resemblance, the skull of her husband or her child which lies in this group, and there seldom passes a day that she does not visit it with a dish of the best-cooked food that her wigwam affords, which she sets before the skull at night, and returns for the dish in the morning. As soon as it is discovered that the sage on which the skull rests is beginning to decay, the woman cuts a fresh bunch and places the skull carefully upon it, removing that which was under it.

"Independent of the above-named duties, which draw the women to this spot, they visit it from inclination, and linger upon it to hold converse and company with the dead. There is scarcely an hour in a pleasant day but more or less of these women may be seen sitting or lying by the skull of their child or husband, talking to it in the most pleasant and endearing language that they can use (as they were wont to do in former days), and seemingly getting an answer back."

From these accounts it may be seen that the peculiar customs which have been described by the authors cited were not confined to any special tribe or area of country, although they do not appear to have prevailed among the Indians of the northwest coast, so far as known.

SUPERTERRENE AND AERIAL BURIAL IN CANOES

THE next mode of burial to be remarked is that of deposit in canoes, either supported on posts, on the ground, or swung from trees, and is common only to the tribes inhabiting the northwest coast. From a number of examples, the following, relating to the Clallams and furnished by the Rev. M. Eells, missionary to the Skokomish Agency, Washington Territory, is selected:

"The deceased was a woman about thirty or thirty-five years of age, dead of consumption. She died in the morning, and in the afternoon I went to the house to attend the funeral. She had then been placed in a Hudson's Bay Company's box for a coffin, which was about 3 1/2 feet long, 1 3/4 wide, and 1 1/2 high. She was very poor when she died, owing to her disease, or she could not have been put in this box. A fire was burning near by, where a large number of her things had been consumed, and the rest were in three boxes near the coffin. Her mother sang the mourning song, sometimes with others, and often saying. 'My daughter, my daughter, why did you die?' and similar words. The burial did not take place until the next day, and I was invited to go. It was an aerial burial, in a canoe. The canoe was about 25 feet long. The posts, of old Indian hewed boards, were about a foot wide. Holes were cut in these, in which boards were placed, on which the canoe rested. One thing I noticed while this was done which was new to me, but the significance of which I did not learn. As fast as the holes were cut in the posts green leaves were gathered and placed over the holes until the posts were put in the ground. The coffin-box and the three others containing her things were placed in the canoe and a roof of boards made over the central part, which was entirely covered with white cloth. The head part and the foot part of her bedstead were then nailed on to the posts, which front the water, and a dress nailed on each of these. After pronouncing the benediction, all left the hill and went to the beach except her father, mother, and brother, who remained ten or fifteen minutes, pounding on the canoe and mourning. They then came down and made a present to those persons who were there--a gun to me, a blanket to each of two or three others, and a dollar and a half to each of the rest, there being about fifteen persons present. Three or four of them then made short speeches, and we came home.

"The reason why she was buried thus is said to be because she is a prominent woman in the tribe. In about nine months it is expected that there will be a 'pot-latch' or distribution of money near this place, and as each tribe shall come they will send a delegation of two or three men, who will carry a present and leave it at the grave; soon after that shall be done she will be buried in the ground. Shortly after her death both her father and mother cut off their hair as a sign of their grief."

George Gibbs [1] gives a most interesting account of the burial ceremonies of the Indians of Oregon and Washington Territory, which is here reproduced in its entirety, although it contains examples of other modes of burial besides that in canoes; but to separate the narrative would destroy the thread of the story:

"The common mode of disposing of the dead among the fishing tribes was in canoes. These were generally drawn into the woods at some prominent point a short distance from the village, and sometimes placed between the forks of trees or raised from the ground on posts. Upon the Columbia River the Tsinuk had in particular two very noted cemeteries, a high isolated bluff about three miles below the mouth of the Cowlitz, called Mount Coffin, and one some distance above, called Coffin Rock. The former would appear not to have been very ancient. Mr. Broughton, one of Vancouver's lieutenants, who explored the river, makes mention only of several canoes at this place; and Lewis and Clarke, who noticed the mount, do not speak of them at all, but at the time of Captain Wilkes's expedition it is conjectured that there were at least 3,000. A fire caused by the carelessness of one of his party destroyed the whole, to the great indignation of the Indians.

"Captain Belcher, of the British ship Sulphur, who visited the river in 1839, remarks: 'In the year 1836 [1826] the small-pox made great ravages, and it was followed a few years since by the ague. Consequently Corpse Island and Coffin Mount, as well as the adjacent shores, were studded not only with canoes, but at the period of our visit the skulls and skeletons were strewed about in all directions.' This method generally prevailed on the neighboring coasts, as at Shoal Water Bay, etc. Farther up the Columbia, as

---

[1] Cont. N. A. Ethnol. 1877, I, p. 200.

at the Cascades, a different form was adopted, which is thus described by Captain Clarke:

"About half a mile below this house, in a very thick part of the woods, is an ancient Indian burial-place; it consists of eight vaults, made of pine or cedar boards, closely connected, about eight feet square and six in height, the top securely covered with wide boards, sloping a little, so as to convey off the rain. The direction of all these is east and west, the door being on the eastern side, and partially stopped with wide boards, decorated with rude pictures of men and other animals. On entering we found in some of them four dead bodies, carefully wrapped in skins, tied with cords of grass and bark, lying on a mat in a direction east and west, the other vaults contained only bones, which in some of them were piled to a height of four feet; on the tops of the vaults and on poles attached to them hung brass kettles and frying-pans with holes in their bottoms, baskets, bowls, sea-shells, skins, pieces of cloth, hair bags of trinkets, and small bones, the offerings of friendship or affection, which have been saved by a pious veneration from the ferocity of war or the more dangerous temptation of individual gain. The whole of the walls as well as the door were decorated with strange figures cut and painted on them, and besides these were several wooden images of men, some of them so old and decayed as to have almost lost their shape, which were all placed against the sides of the vault. These images, as well as those in the houses we have lately seen, do not appear to be at all the objects of adoration in this place; they were most probably intended as resemblances of those whose decease they indicate; and when we observe them in houses they occupy the most conspicuous part, but are treated more like ornaments than objects of worship. Near the vaults which are still standing are the remains of others on the ground, completely rotted and covered with moss; and as they are formed of the most durable pine and cedar timber, there is every appearance that for a very long series of years this retired spot has been the depository for the Indians near this place."

"Another depository of this kind upon an island in the river a few miles above gave it the name of Sepulcher Island. The Watlala, a tribe of the Upper Tsinuk, whose burial place is here described, are now nearly extinct; but a number of the sepulchers still remain in different states of preservation. The position of the body, as noticed by Clarke, is, I believe, of universal observance, the head being always placed to the west. The reason assigned to me is that the road to the me-mel-us-illa-hee, the country of the dead, is toward the west, and if they place them otherwise they would be confused. East of the Cascade Mountains the tribes whose habits are equestrian, and who use canoes only for ferriage or transportation purposes, bury their dead, usually heaping over them piles of stones, either to mark the spot or to prevent the bodies from being exhumed by the prairie wolf. Among the Yakamas we saw many of their graves placed in conspicuous points of the basaltic walls which line the lower valleys, and designated by a clump of poles planted over them, from which fluttered various articles of dress. Formerly these prairie tribes killed horses over the graves--a custom now falling into disuse in consequence of the teachings of the whites.

"Upon Puget Sound all the forms obtain in different localities. Among the Makah of Cape Flattery the graves are covered with a sort of box, rudely constructed of boards, and else where on the Sound the same method is adopted in some cases, while in others the bodies are placed on elevated scaffolds. As a general thing, however, the Indians upon the water placed the dead in canoes, while those at a distance from it buried them. Most of the graves are surrounded with strips of cloth, blankets, and other articles of property. Mr. Cameron, an English gentleman residing at Esquimalt Harbor, Vancouver Island, informed me that on his place there were graves having at each corner a large stone, the interior space filled with rubbish. The origin of these was unknown to the present Indians.

"The distinctions of rank or wealth in all cases were very marked; persons of no consideration and slaves being buried with very little care or respect. Vancouver, whose attention was particularly attracted to their methods of disposing of the dead, mentions that at Port Discovery he saw baskets suspended to the trees containing the skeletons of young children, and, what is not easily explained, small square boxes, containing, apparently, food. I do not think that any of these tribes place articles of food with the dead, nor have I been able to learn from living Indians that they formerly followed that practice. What he took for such I do not understand. He also mentions seeing in the same place a cleared space recently burned over, in which the skulls and bones of a number lay among the ashes. The practice of burning the dead exists in parts of California and among the Tshimsyan of Fort Simpson. It is also pursued by the "Carriers" of New California, but no intermediate tribes, to my knowledge, follow it. Certainly those of the Sound do not at present.

"It is clear from Vancouver's narrative that some great epidemic had recently passed through the country, as manifested by the quantity of human remains uncared for and exposed at the time of his visit, and very probably the Indians, being afraid, had burned a house, in which the inhabitants had perished with the dead in it. This is frequently done. They almost invariably remove from an place where sickness has prevailed, generally destroying the house also.

"At Penn Cove Mr. Whidbey, one of Vancouver's officers, noticed several sepulchers formed exactly like a sentry-box. Some of them were open, and contained the skeletons, of many young children tied up in baskets. The smaller bones of adults were likewise noticed, but not one of the limb bones was found; which gave rise to an opinion that these, by the living inhabitants of the neighborhood, were appropriated to useful purposes, such as pointing their arrows, spears, or other weapons.

"It is hardly necessary to say that such a practice is altogether foreign to Indian character. The bones of the adults had probably been removed and buried elsewhere. The corpses of children are variously disposed of; sometimes by suspending them, at others by placing in the hollows of trees, A cemetery devoted to infants is, however, an unusual occurrence. In cases of chiefs or men of note much pomp was used in the accompaniments of the rite. The canoes were of great size and value--the war or state canoes of the deceased. Frequently one was inverted over that holding the body, and in one instance, near Shoalwater Bay, the corpse was deposited in a small canoe, which again was placed in a larger one and covered with a third. Among the Tsinuk and Tsihalis the tamahno-us board of the owner was placed near him. The Puget Sound Indians do not make these tamahno-us hoards, but they sometimes constructed effigies of their chiefs, resembling the person as nearly as possible, dressed in his usual costume, and wearing the articles of which he was fond. One of these, representing the Skagit chief Sneestum, stood very conspicuously upon a high bank on the eastern side of Whidbey Island The figures observed by Captain Clarke at the Cascades were either of this description or else the carved, posts which had ornamented the interior of the houses of the deceased, and were connected with the superstition of the tamahno-us. The most valuable articles of property were put into or hung up around the grave, being first carefully rendered unserviceable, and the living family were literally stripped to do honor to the dead. No little self-denial must have been practiced in parting with articles so precious, but those interested frequently had the least to say on the subject. The graves of women were distinguished by a cup, a Kamas stick, or other implement of their occupation, and by articles of dress.

"Slaves were killed in proportion to the rank and wealth of the deceased. In some instances they were starved to death, or even tied to the dead body and left to perish thus horribly. At present this practice has been almost entirely given up, but till within a very few years it was not uncommon. A case which occurred in 1850 has been already mentioned. Still later, in 1853, Toke, a Tsinuk chief living at Shoalwater Bay, undertook to kill a slave girl belonging to his daughter, who, in dying, had requested that this might be done. The woman fled, and was found by some citizens in the woods half starved. Her master attempted to reclaim her, but was soundly thrashed and warned against another attempt.

"It was usual in the case of chiefs to renew or repair for a considerable length of time the materials and ornaments of the burial- place. With the common class of persons family pride or domestic affection was satisfied with the gathering together of the bones after the flesh had decayed and wrapping them in a new mat. The violation of the grave was always regarded as an offense of the first magnitude and provoked severe revenge. Captain Belcher remarks, 'Great secrecy is observed in all their burial ceremonies, partly from fear of Europeans, and as among themselves they will instantly punish by death any violation of the tomb or wage war if perpetrated by another tribe, so they are inveterate and tenaciously bent on revenge should they discover that any act of the kind has been perpetrated by a white man. It is on record that part of the crew of a vessel on her return to this port (the Columbia) suffered because a person who belonged to her (but not then in her) was known to have taken a skull, which, from the process of flattening, had become an object of curiosity.' He adds, however, that at the period of his visit to the river 'the skulls and skeletons were scattered about in all directions; and as I was on most of their positions unnoticed by the natives, I suspect the feeling does not extend much beyond their relatives, and then only till decay has destroyed body, goods, and chattels. The chiefs, no doubt, are watched, as their canoes are repainted, decorated, and greater care taken by placing them in sequestered spots.'

"The motive for sacrificing or destroying property on occasion of death will be referred to in treating of their religious ideas. Wailing for the dead is continued for a long time, and seems to be rather a ceremonial performance than an act of spontaneous grief. The duty, of course, belongs to the woman, and the early morning is usually chosen for the purpose. They go out alone to some place a little distant from the lodge or camp, and in a loud, sobbing voice repeat a sort of stereotyped formula, as, for instance, a mother, on the loss of her child, 'Ah seahb shed-da bud-dah ah ta bud! ad-de- dah, Ah chief!' 'My child dead, alas!' When in dreams they see any of their deceased friends this lamentation is renewed."

With most of the Northwest Indians it was quite common, as mentioned by Mr. Gibbs, to kill or bury with the dead a living slave, who, failing to die within three days was strangled by another slave, but the custom has also prevailed among other tribes and peoples, in many cases the individuals offering themselves as voluntary sacrifices. Bancroft states "that in Panama, Nata, and some other districts, when a cacique died those of his concubines that loved him enough, those that he loved ardently and so appointed, as well as certain servants, killed themselves and were interred with him. This they did in order that they might wait upon him in the land of spirits." It is well known to all readers of history to what an extreme this revolting practice has prevailed in Mexico, South America, and Africa.

AQUATIC BURIAL

AS a confirmed rite or ceremony, this mode of disposing of the dead has never been followed by any of our North American Indians, although occasionally the dead have been disposed of by sinking in springs or watercourses, by throwing into the sea, or by setting afloat in canoes. Among the nations of antiquity the practice was not uncommon, for we are informed that the Ichtliyophagi, or fish-eaters, mentioned by Ptolemy, living in a region bordering on the Persian Gulf, invariably committed their dead to the sea, thus repaying the obligations they had incurred to its inhabitants. The Lotophagians did the same, and the Hyperboreans, with a commendable degree of forethought for the survivors, when ill or about to die, threw themselves into the sea. The burial of Baldor "the beautiful," it may be remembered, was in a highly decorated ship, which was pushed down to the sea, set on fire, and committed to the waves. The Itzas of Guatemala, living on the islands of Lake Peter, according to Bancroft, are said to have thrown their dead into the lake for want of room. The Indiana of Nootka Sound and the Chinooks were in the habit of thus getting rid of their dead slaves, and, according to Timberlake, the Cherokees of Tennessee "seldom bury the dead, but threw them into the river."

After a careful search for well-authenticated instances of burial, aquatic and semi-aquatic, but two have been found, which are here given. The first relates to the Gosh-Utes, and is by Capt J. H. Simpson: [1]

"Skull Valley, which is a part of the Great Salt Lake Desert, and which we have crossed to-day, Mr. George W. Bean, my guide over this route last fall, says derives its name from the number of skulls which have been found in it, and which have arisen from the custom of the Goshute Indians burying their dead in springs, which they sink with stones or keep down with sticks. He says he has actually seen the Indians bury their dead in this way near the town of Provo, where he resides."

---

[1] Exploration Great Salt Lake Valley, Utah, 1859, p. 48.

As corroboration of this statement, Captain Simpson mentions in another part of the volume that, arriving at a spring one evening, they were obliged to dig out the skeleton of an Indian from the mud at the bottom before using the water.

This peculiar mode of burial is entirely unique, so far as known, and but from the well-known probity of the relator might well be questioned, especially when it is remembered that in the country spoken of water is quite scarce and Indians are careful not to pollute the streams or springs near which they live. Conjecture seems useless to establish a reason for this disposition of the dead.

The second example is by Catlin [1] and relates to the Chinook.

"... This little cradle has a strap which passes over the woman's forehead whilst the cradle rides on her back, and if the child dies during its subjection to this rigid mode its cradle becomes its coffin, forming a little canoe, in which it lie floating on the water in some sacred pool, where they are often in the habit of fastening their canoes containing the dead bodies of the old and young, or, which is often the case, elevated into the branches of trees, where their bodies are left to decay and their bones to dry whilst they are bandaged in man skins and ominously packed in their canoes, with paddles to propel and ladles to bail them out, and provisions to last and pipes to smoke as they are performing their 'long journey after death to their contemplated hunting grounds,' which these people think is to be performed in their canoes."

---

[1] Hist. North American Indians, 1844, II, p. 141

LIVING SEPULCHERS

THIS is a term quaintly used by the learned M Pierre Muret to express the devouring of the dead by birds and animals or the surviving friends and relatives. Exposure of the dead to animals and birds has already been mentioned, but in the absence of any positive proof it is not believed that the North American Indians followed the custom, although cannibalism may have prevailed to a limited extent. It is true that a few accounts are given by authors, but these are considered to be so apochryphal in character that for the present it is deemed prudential to omit them. That such a means of disposing of the dead was not in practice is somewhat remarkable when we take into consideration how many analogies have been found in comparing old and new world funeral observances, and the statements made by Bruhier, Lafitau, Muret, and others, who give a number of examples of this peculiar mode of burial.

For instance, the Tartars sometimes ate their dead, and the Massageties, Derbices, and Effedens did the same, having previously strangled the aged and mixed their flesh with mutton. Horace and Tertulian both affirm that the Irish and ancient Britons devoured the dead, and Lafitau remarks that certain Indians of South America did the same, esteeming this mode of disposal more honorable and much to be preferred than to rot and be eaten by worms. To the credit of our savages, this barbarous and revolting practice is not believed to have been practiced by them.

MOURNING, FEASTS, FOOD, DANCES, SONGS, GAMES, POSTS, FIRES, AND SUPERSTITIONS IN CONNECTION WITH BURIAL

THE above subjects are coincidental with burial, and some of them, particularly mourning, have been more or less treated of in this paper, yet it may be of advantage to here give a few of the collected examples, under separate heads.

MOURNING

One of the most carefully described scenes of mourning at the death of a chief of the Crows is related in the life of Beckwourth,[1] who for many years lived among this people, finally attaining great distinction as a warrior.

"I dispatched a herald to the village to inform them of the head chief's death, and then, burying him according to his directions, we slowly proceeded homewards. My very soul sickened at the contemplation of the scenes that would be enacted at my arrival. When we drew in sight of the village, we found every lodge laid prostrate. We entered amid shrieks, cries, and yells. Blood was streaming from every conceivable part of the bodies of all who were old enough to comprehend their loss. Hundreds of fingers were dismembered; hair torn from the head lay in profusion about the paths, wails and moans in every direction assailed the ear, where unrestrained joy had a few hours before prevailed. This fearful mourning lasted until evening of the next day....

"A herald having been dispatched to our other villages to acquaint them with the death of our head chief and request them to assemble at the Rose Bud in order to meet our village and devote themselves to a general time of mourning there met in conformity with this summons over ten thousand Crows at the place indicated. Such a scene of disorderly vociferous mourning no imagination can conceive nor any pen portray. Long Hair cut off a large roll of his hair, a thing he was never known to do before. The

---

[1] Autobiography of James Beckwourth, 1856, p. 260.

cutting and hacking of human flesh exceeded all my previous experience; fingers were dismembered as readily as twigs, and blood was poured out like water. Many of the warriors would cut two gashes nearly the entire length of their arm, then separating the skin from the flesh at one end, would grasp it in their other hand and rip it asunder to the shoulder. Others would carve various devices upon their breasts and shoulders and raise the skin in the same manner to make the scars show to advantage after the wound was healed. Some of their mutilations were ghastly and my heart sickened to look at them, but they would not appear to receive any pain from them."

From I. L. Mahan, United States Indian Agent for the Chippewas of Lake Superior, Red Cliff, Wisconsin, the following detailed account of mourning has been received.

There is probably no people that exhibit more sorrow and grief for their dead than they. The young widow mourns the loss of her husband; by day as by night she is heard silently sobbing; she is a constant visitor to the place of rest; with the greatest reluctance will she follow the raised camp. The friends and relatives of the young mourner will incessantly devise methods to distract her mind from the thought of her lost husband. She refuses nourishment but as nature is exhausted she is prevailed upon to partake of food; the supply is scant, but on every occasion the best and largest proportion is deposited upon the grave of her husband. In the mean time the female relatives of the deceased have according to custom submitted to her charge a parcel made up of different cloths ornamented with bead-work and eagles' feathers which she is charged to keep by her side--the place made vacant by the demise of her husband--a reminder of her widowhood. She is therefore for a term of twelve moons not permitted to wear any finery, neither is she permitted to slicken up and comb her head; this to avoid attracting attention. Once in a while a female relative of deceased, commiserating with her grief and sorrow, will visit her and voluntarily proceed to comb out the long-neglected and matted hair. With a jealous eye a vigilant watch is kept over her conduct during the term of her widowhood, yet she is allowed the privilege to marry, any time during her widowhood, an unmarried brother or cousin, or a person of the same Dodem [sic] (family mark) of her husband.

"At the expiration of her term, the vows having been faithfully performed and kept, the female relatives of deceased assemble and, with greetings commensurate to the occasion, proceed to wash her face, comb her hair, and attire her person with new apparel, and otherwise demonstrating the release from her vow and restraint. Still she has not her entire freedom. If she will still refuse to marry a relative of the deceased and will marry another, she then has to purchase her freedom by giving a certain amount of goods and whatever else she might have manufactured during her widowhood in anticipation of the future now at hand. Frequently, though, during widowhood the vows are disregarded and an inclination to flirt and play courtship or form an alliance of marriage outside of the relatives of the deceased is being indulged, and when discovered the widow is set upon by the female relatives, her slick braided hair is shorn close up to the back of her neck, all her apparel and trinkets are torn from her person, and a quarrel frequently results fatally to some member of one or the other side."

The substitution of a reminder for the dead husband, made from rags, furs, and other articles, is not confined alone to the Chippewas, other tribes having the same custom. In some instances the widows are obliged to carry around with them, for a variable period, a bundle containing the bones of the deceased consort.

Benson [1] gives the following account of their funeral ceremonies, embracing the disposition of the body, mourning feast and dance:

"Their funeral is styled by them 'the last cry.'

"When the husband dies the friends assemble, prepare the grave, and place the corpse in it, but do not fill it up. The gun, bow and arrows, hatchet and knife are deposited in the grave. Poles are planted at the head and the foot, upon which flags are placed; the grave is then enclosed by pickets driven in the ground. The funeral ceremonies now begin, the widow being the chief mourner. At night and morning she will go to the grave and pour forth the most piteous cries and wailings. It is not important that any other member of the family should take any very active part in the 'cry,' though they do participate to some extent.

"The widow wholly neglects her toilet, while she daily goes to the grave during one entire moon from the date when the death occurred. On the

---

[1] Life among the Choctaws, 1860, p. 294.

evening of the last day of the moon the friends all assemble at the cabin of the disconsolate widow, bringing provisions for a sumptuous feast, which consists of corn and jerked beef boiled together in a kettle. While the supper is preparing, the bereaved wife goes to the grave, and pours out, with unusual vehemence, her bitter wailings and lamentations. When the food is thoroughly cooked the kettle is taken from the fire and placed in the center of the cabin, and the friends gather around it, passing the buffalo-horn spoon from hand to hand and from mouth to mouth till all have been bountifully supplied. While supper is being served, two of the oldest men of the company quietly withdraw and go to the grave and fill it up, taking down the flags. All then join in a dance, which not unfrequently is continued till morning; the widow does not fail to unite in the dance, and to contribute her part to the festivities of the occasion. This is the 'last cry,' the days of mourning are ended, and the widow is now ready to form another matrimonial alliance. The ceremonies are precisely the same when a man has lost his wife, and they are only slightly varied when any other member of the family has died. (Slaves were buried without ceremonies.)"

FEASTS

In Beltrami [1] an account is given of the funeral ceremonies of one of the tribes of the west, including a description of the feast which took place before the body was consigned to its final resting place:

"I was a spectator of the funeral ceremony performed in honor of the manes of Cloudy Weather's son-in-law, whose body had remained with the Sioux, and was suspected to have furnished one of their repasts. What appeared not a little singular and indeed ludicrous in this funeral comedy was the contrast exhibited by the terrific lamentations and yells of one part of the company while the others were singing and dancing with all their might.

"At another funeral ceremony for a member of the Grand Medicine, and at which as a man of another world I was permitted to attend, the same practice occurred. But at the feast which took place on that occasion an allowance was served up for the deceased out of every article of which it consisted, while others were beating, wounding, and torturing themselves, and letting their blood flow both over the dead man and his provisions,

---

[1] Pilgrimage, 1828, ii, p. 443.

thinking possibly that this was the most palatable seasoning for the latter which they could possibly supply. His wife furnished out an entertainment present for him of all her hair and rags, with which, together with his arms, his provisions, his ornaments, and his mystic medicine bag, he was wrapped up in the skin which had been his last covering when alive. He was then tied round with the bark of some particular trees which they use for making cords, and bonds of a very firm texture and hold (the only ones indeed which they have), and instead of being buried in the earth was hung up to a large oak. The reason of this was that, as his favorite Manitou was the eagle, his spirit would be enabled more easily from such a situation to fly with him to Paradise."

Hind [1] mentions an account of a burial feast by De Brebeuf which occurred among the Hurons of New York:

"The Jesuit missionary, P. de Brebeuf, who assisted at one of the 'feasts of the dead' at the village of Ossosane, before the dispersion of the Hurons, relates that the ceremony took place in the presence of 2,000 Indians, who offered 1,200 presents at the common tomb, in testimony of their grief. The people belonging to five large villages deposited the bones of their dead in a gigantic shroud, composed of forty-eight robes, each robe being made of ten beaver skins. After being carefully wrapped in this shroud, they were placed between moss and bark. A wall of stones was built around this vast ossuary to preserve it from profanation. Before covering the bones with earth a few grains of Indian corn were thrown by the women upon the sacred relics. According to the superstitious belief of the Hurons the souls of the dead remain near the bodies until the 'feast of the dead'; after which ceremony they become free, and can at once depart for the land of spirits, which they believe to be situated in the regions of the setting sun."

SUPERSTITION REGARDING BURIAL FEASTS

The following account is by Dr. S G. Wright, acting physician to the Leech Lake Agency, Minnesota:

"Pagan Indians, or those who have not become Christians, still adhere to the ancient practice of feasting at the grave of departed friends; the object

---

[1] Canadian Red River Exploring Expedition, 1860, ii, p. 164.

is to feast with the departed; that is, they believe that while they partake of the visible material the departed spirit partakes at the same time of the spirit that dwells in the food. From ancient time it was customary to bury with the dead various articles, such especially as were most valued in lifetime. The idea was that there was a spirit dwelling in the article represented by the material article; thus the war-club contained a spiritual war-club, the pipe a spiritual pipe, which could be used by the departed in another world. These several spiritual implements were supposed, of course, to accompany the soul, to be used also on the way to its final abode. This habit has now ceased...."

FOOD

This subject has been sufficiently mentioned elsewhere in connection with other matters and does not need to be now repeated. It has been an almost universal custom throughout the whole extent of the country to place food in or near the grave of deceased persons.

DANCES

Gymnastic exercises, dignified with this name, upon the occasion of a death or funeral, were common to many tribes. It is thus described by Morgan: [1]

"An occasional and very singular figure was called the 'dance for the dead' It was known as the O-he-wa. It was danced by the women alone. The music was entirely vocal, a select band of singers being stationed in the center of the room. To the songs for the dead which they sang the dancers joined in chorus. It was plaintive and mournful music. This dance was usually separate from all councils and the only dance of the occasion. It commenced at dusk or soon after and continued until towards morning, when the shades of the dead who were believed to be present and participate in the dance were supposed to disappear. This dance was had whenever a family which had lost a member called for it, which was usually a year after the event. In the spring and fall it was often given for all the dead indiscriminately, who were believed then to revisit the earth and join in the dance."

---

[1] League of the Iroquois, 1851, p. 297.

The interesting account which now follows is by Stephen Powers, [1] and relates to the Yo-kai-a of California, containing other matters of importance pertaining to burial.

"I paid a visit to their camp four miles below Ukiah, and finding there a unique kind of assembly-house, desired to enter and examine it, but was not allowed to do so until I had gained the confidence of the old sexton by a few friendly words and the tender of a silver half dollar. The pit of it was about 50 feet in diameter and 4 or 5 feet deep, and it was so heavily roofed with earth that the interior was damp and somber as a tomb. It looked like a low tumulus, and was provided with a tunnel-like entrance about 10 feet long and 4 feet high, and leading down to a level with the floor of the pit. The mouth of the tunnel was closed with brush, and the venerable sexton would not remove it until he had slowly and devoutly paced several times to and fro before the entrance.

"Passing in I found the massive roof supported by a number of peeled poles painted white and ringed with black and ornamented with rude devices. The floor was covered thick and green with sprouting wheat, which had been scattered to feed the spirit of the captain of the tribe, lately deceased. Not long afterward a deputation of the Senel came up to condole with the Yo-kai-a on the loss of their chief, and a dance or series of dances was held which lasted three days. During this time of course the Senel were the guests of the Yo-kai-a, and the latter were subjected to a considerable expense. I was prevented by other engagements from being present, and shall be obliged to depend on the description of an eye-witness, Mr. John Tenney, whose account is here given with a few changes.

"There are four officials connected with the building, who are probably chosen to preserve order and to allow no intruders. They are the assistants of the chief. The invitation to attend was from one of them, and admission was given by the same. These four wore black vests trimmed with red flannel and shell ornaments. The chief made no special display on the occasion. In addition to these four, who were officers of the assembly-chamber, there was an old man and a young woman, who seemed to be priest and priestess. The young woman was dressed differently from any other, the rest dressing in plain calico dresses. Her dress was white covered with spots of red flannel, cut in neat figures, ornamented with shells. It

---

[1] Cont. to North American Ethnol., 1878, iv, p. 164.

looked gorgeous and denoted some office, the name of which I could not ascertain. Before the visitors were ready to enter, the older men of the tribe were reclining around the fire smoking and chatting. As the ceremonies were about to commence, the old man and young woman were summoned, and, standing at the end opposite the entrance, they inaugurated the exercises by a brief service, which seemed to be a dedication of the house to the exercises about to commence. Each of them spoke a few words, joined in a brief chant, and the house was thrown open for their visitors. They staid at their post until the visitors entered and were seated on one side of the room. After the visitors then others were seated, making about 200 in all, though there was plenty of room in the center for the dancing.

"Before the dance commenced the chief of the visiting tribe made a brief speech, in which he no doubt referred to the death of the chief of the Yo-kai-a, and offered the sympathy of his tribe in this loss. As he spoke, some of the women scarcely refrained from crying out, and with difficulty they suppressed their sobs. I presume that he proposed a few moments of mourning, for when he stopped the whole assemblage burst forth into a bitter wailing, some screaming as if in agony. The whole thing created such a din that I was compelled to stop my ears. The air was rent and pierced with their cries. This wailing and shedding of tears lasted about three or five minutes, though it seemed to last a half hour. At a given signal they ceased, wiped their eyes, and quieted down.

"Then preparations were made for the dance. One end of the room was set aside for the dressing-room. The chief actors were five men, who were muscular and agile. They were profusely decorated with paint and feathers, while white and dark stripes covered their bodies. They were girt about the middle with cloth of bright colors, sometimes with variegated shawls. A feather mantle hung from the shoulder, reaching below the knee; strings of shells ornamented the neck, while their heads were covered with a crown of eagle feathers. They had whistles in their mouths as they danced, swaying their heads, bending and whirling their bodies; every muscle seemed to be exercised, and the feather ornaments quivered with light. They were agile and graceful as they bounded about in the sinuous course of the dance.

"The five men were assisted by a semicircle of twenty women, who only marked time by stepping up and down with short step; they always took their places first and disappeared first, the men making their exit gracefully one by one. The dresses of the women were suitable for the occasion. They were white dresses trimmed heavily with black velvet. The stripes were about three inches wide, some plain and others edged like saw-teeth. This was an indication of their mourning for the dead chief in whose honor they had prepared that style of dancing. Strings of haliotis and pachydesma shell beads encircled their necks, and around their waists were belts heavily loaded with the same material. Their head-dresses were more showy than those of the men. The head was encircled with a bandeau of otters' or beavers' fur, to which were attached short wires standing out in all directions, with glass or shell beads strung on them, and at the tips little feather flags and quail plumes. Surmounting all was a pyramidal plume of feathers, black, gray, and scarlet, the top generally being a bright scarlet bunch, waving and tossing very beautifully. All these combined gave their heads a very brilliant and spangled appearance.

"The first day the dance was slow and funereal, in honor of the Yo- kai-a chief who died a short time before. The music was mournful and simple being a monotonous chant in which only two tones were used, accompanied with a rattling of split sticks and stamping on a hollow slab. The second day the dance was more lively on the part of the men, the music was better, employing airs which had a greater range of tune and the women generally joined in the chorus. The dress of the women was not so beautiful as they appeared in ordinary calico. The third day if observed in accordance with Indian custom the dancing was still more lively and the proceedings more gay just as the coming home from a Christian funeral is apt to be much more jolly than the going out."

A Yo-kai-a widow's style of mourning is peculiar. In addition to the usual evidences of grief she mingles the ashes of her dead husband with pitch making a white tar or unguent, with which she smears a band about two inches wide all around the edge of the hair (which is previously cut off close to the head) so that at a little distance she appears to be wearing a white chaplet.

It is their custom to feed the spirits of the dead for the space of one year by going daily to places which they were accustomed to frequent while living, where they sprinkle pinole upon the ground. A Yo-kai-a mother who has lost her babe goes every day for a year to some place where her little one played when alive or to the spot where the body was burned and milks her breasts into the air. This is accompanied by plaintive mourning and weeping and piteous calling upon her little one to return and sometimes she sings a hoarse and melancholy chant and dances with a wild ecstatic swaying of her body.

SONGS

It has nearly always been customary to sing songs at not only funerals but for varying periods of time afterwards although these chants may no doubt occasionally have been simply wailing or mournful ejaculation. A writer [1] mentions it as follows:

"At almost all funerals there is an irregular crying kind of singing with no accompaniments, but generally all do not sing the same melody at the same time in unison. Several may sing the same song and at the same time, but each begins and finishes when he or she may wish. Often for weeks, or even months, after the decease of a dear friend, a living one, usually a woman, will sit by her house and sing or cry by the hour; and they also sing for a short time when they visit the grave or meet an esteemed friend whom they have not seen since the decease. At the funeral both men and women sing. No. 11 I have heard more frequently some time after the funeral, and No. 12 at the time of the funeral, by the Twanas (For song see p. 251.) The words are simply an exclamation of grief, as our word 'alas'; but they also have other words which they use, and sometimes they use merely the syllable la. Often the notes are sung in this order, and sometimes not, but in some order the notes do and la, and occasionally mi, are sung."

GAMES

It is not proposed to describe under this heading examples of those athletic and gymnastic performances following the death of a person which have been described by Lafitau, but simply to call attention to a practice as a secondary or adjunct part of the funeral rites, which consists in gambling for the possession of the property of the defunct. Dr. Charles E. McChesney, U. S. A., who for some time was stationed among the Wahpeton and Sisseton Sioux, furnishes a detailed and interesting account of what is

---

[1] Am. Antiq., April-May-June 1879, p. 251.

called the "ghost gamble." This is played with marked wild-plum stones. So far as ascertained it is peculiar to the Sioux.

"After the death of a wealthy Indian the near relatives take charge of the effects, and at a stated time--usually at the time of the first feast held over the bundle containing the lock of hair--they are divided into many small piles, so as to give all the Indians invited to play an opportunity to win something. One Indian is selected to represent the ghost, and he plays against all the others, who are not required to stake anything on the result, but simply invited to take part in the ceremony, which is usually held in the lodge of the dead person, in which is contained the bundle inclosing the lock of hair. In cases where the ghost himself is not wealthy the stakes are furnished by his rich friends, should he have any. The players are called in one at a time, and play singly against the ghost's representative, the gambling being done in recent years by means of cards. If the invited player succeeds in beating the ghost he takes one of the piles of goods and passes out when another is invited to play, etc., until all the piles of goods are won. In cases of men only the men play and in cases of women the women only take part in the ceremony."

Before the white men came among these Indians and taught them many of his improved vices this game was played by means of figured plum seeds, the men using eight and the women seven seeds figured as follows:

"Two seeds are simply blackened on one side the reverse containing nothing. Two seeds are black on one side with a small spot of the color of the seed left in the center, the reverse side having a black spot in the center, the body being plain. Two seeds have a buffalo's head on one side and the reverse simply two crossed black lines. There is but one seed of this kind in the set used by the women. Two seeds have half of one side blackened and the rest left plain so as to represent a half moon, the reverse has a black longitudinal line crossed at right angles by six small ones. There are six throws whereby the player can win and five that entitle him to another throw. The winning throws are as follows, each winner taking a pile of the ghost's goods:

"Two plain ones up, two plain with black spots up, Buffalo's head up, and two half moons up wins a pile. Two plain black ones up, two black with natural spot up, two longitudinally crossed ones up, and the transversely crossed one up wins a pile. Two plain black ones up, two black with natural spots up, two half moons up, and the transversely crossed one up wins a pile. Two plain black ones, two black with natural spot up, two half moons up, and the buffalo's head up wins a pile. Two plain ones up, two with black spots up, two longitudinally crossed ones up, and the transversely crossed one up wins a pile. Two plain ones up, two with black spots up, buffalo's head up, and two long crossed up wins a pile. The following throws entitle to another chance to win: two plain ones up, two with black spots up, one half moon up, one longitudinally crossed one up, and Buffalo's head up gives another throw, and on this throw if the two plain ones up and two with black spots with either of the half moons or Buffalo's head up, the player takes a pile. Two plain ones up, two with black spots up, two half moons up, and the transversely crossed one up entitles to another throw, when, if all of the black sides come up excepting one, the throw wins. One of the plain ones up and all the rest with black sides up gives another throw, and the same then turning up wins. One of the plain black ones up with that side up of all the others having the least black on gives another throw, when the same turning up again wins. One half moon up with that side up of all the others having the least black on gives another throw, and if the throw is then duplicated it wins. The eighth seed, used by the men has its place in their game whenever its facings are mentioned above. I transmit with this paper a set of these figured seeds, which can be used to illustrate the game if desired. These seeds are said to be nearly a hundred years old, and sets of them are now very rare."

For assisting in obtaining this account Dr. McChesney acknowledges his indebtedness to Dr C. C. Miller, physician to the Sisseton Indian Agency.

POSTS

These are placed at the head or foot of the grave, or both, and have painted or carved on them a history of the deceased or his family, certain totemic characters, or, according to Schoolcraft, not the achievements of the dead, but of those warriors who assisted and danced at the interment. The northwest tribes and others frequently plant poles near the graves, suspending therefrom bits of rag flags, horses tails, etc. The custom among the present Indians does not exist to any extent. Beltrami [1] speaks of it as follows.

---

[1] Pilgrimage, 1828, ii, p. 308.

"Here I saw a most singular union. One of these graves was surmounted by a cross, whilst upon another close to it a trunk of a tree was raised, covered with hieroglyphics recording the number of enemies slain by the tenant of the tomb and several of his tutelary Manitous."

FIRES

It is extremely difficult to determine why the custom of building fires on or near graves originated, some authors stating that the soul thereby underwent a certain process of purification, others that demons were driven away by them, and again that they were to afford light to the wandering soul setting out for the spirit land. One writer states that "the Algonkins believed that the fire lighted nightly on the grave was to light the spirit on its journey. By a coincidence to be explained by the universal sacredness of the number, both Algonkins and Mexicans maintained it for four nights consecutively. The former related the tradition that one of their ancestors returned from the spirit land and informed their nation that the journey thither consumed just four days, and that collecting fuel every night added much to the toil and fatigue the soul encountered, all of which could be spared it". So it would appear that the belief existed that the fire was also intended to assist the spirit in preparing its repast. "Stephen Powers [1] gives a tradition current among the Yurok of California as to the use of fires.

"After death they keep a fire burning certain nights in the vicinity of the grave. They hold and believe, at least the 'Big Indians' do, that the spirits of the departed are compelled to cross an extremely attenuated greasy pole, which bridges over the chasm of the debatable land, and that they require the fire to light them on their darksome journey. A righteous soul traverses the pole quicker than a wicked one, hence they regulate the number of nights for burning a light according to the character for goodness or the opposite which the deceased possessed in this world." Dr. Emil Bessels, of the Polaris expedition, informs the writer that a somewhat similar belief obtains among the Esquimaux.

SUPERSTITIONS

---

[1] Cont. to N. A. Ethnol., 1877, ii, p.58

An entire volume might well be written which should embrace only an account of the superstitions regarding death and burial among the Indians, so thoroughly has the matter been examined and discussed by various authors, and yet so much still remains to be commented on, but in this work, which is simply preliminary, and is hoped will be provocative of future efforts, it is deemed sufficient to give only a few accounts. The first is by Dr. W. Mathews, U. S. A., [1] and relates to the Hidatsa:

"When a Hidatsa dies his shade lingers four nights around the camp or village in which he died, and then goes to the lodge of his departed kindred in the 'village of the dead.' When he has arrived there he is rewarded for his valor, self-denial, and ambition on earth by receiving the same regard in the one place as in the other, for there as here the brave man is honored and the coward despised. Some say that the ghosts of those that commit suicide occupy a separate part of the village, but that their condition differs in no wise from that of the others. In the next world human shades hunt and live in the shades of buffalo and other animals that have here died. There, too, there are four seasons, but they come in an inverse order to the terrestrial seasons. During the four nights that the ghost is supposed to linger near his former dwelling, those who disliked or feared the deceased, and do not wish a visit from the shade, scorch with red coals a pair of moccasins which they leave at the door of the lodge. The smell of the burning leather they claim keeps the ghost out; but the true friends of the dead man take no such precautions."

From this account it will be seen that the Hidatsa as well as the Algonkins and Mexicans believed that four days were required before the spirit could finally leave the earth. Why the smell of burning leather should he offensive to spirits it would perhaps be fruitless to speculate on.

The next account, by Keating, [2] relating to the Chippewas, shows a slight analogy regarding the slippery-pole tradition already alluded to:

"The Chippewas believe that there is in man an essence entirely distinct from the body; they call it Ochechag, and appear to supply to it the qualities which we refer to the soul. They believe that it quits the body at the time of death and repairs to what they term Chekechekchekawe; this

---

[1] Ethnol. and Philol. of the Hidatsa Indians. U.S. Geol. Surv. of Terr., 1877, p. 409
[2] Long's Exped., 1824, ii, p. l58.

region is supposed to be situated to the south and on the shores of the great ocean. Previous to arriving there they meet with a stream which they are obliged to cross upon a large snake that answers the purpose of a bridge; those who die from drowning never succeed in crossing the stream; they are thrown into it and remain there forever. Some souls come to the edge of the stream but are prevented from passing by the snake that threatens to devour them: these are the souls of the persons in a lethargy or trance. Being refused a passage, these souls return to their bodies and reanimate them. They believe that animals have souls and even that inorganic substances such as kettles etc., have in them a similar essence."

In this land of souls all are treated according to their merits. Those who have been good men are free from pain, they have no duties to perform, their time is spent in dancing and singing and they feed upon mushrooms which are very abundant The souls of bad men are haunted by the phantom of the persons or things that they have injured, thus if a man has destroyed much property the phantoms of the wrecks of this property obstruct his passage wherever he goes, if he has been cruel to his dogs or horses they also torment him after death. The ghosts of those whom during his lifetime he wronged are there permitted to avenge their injuries. They think that when a soul has crossed the stream it cannot return to its body, yet they believe in apparitions and entertain the opinion that the spirits of the departed will frequently revisit the abodes of their friends in order to invite them to the other world and to forewarn them of their approaching dissolution.

Stephen Powers in his valuable work so often quoted, gives a number of examples of superstitions regarding the dead of which the following relates to the Karok of California.

"How well and truly the Karok reverence the memory of the dead is shown by the fact that the highest crime one can commit is the pet- chi-e-ri, the mere mention of the dead relative's name. It is a deadly insult to the survivors and can be atoned for only by the same amount of blood money paid for willful murder. In default of that they will have the villain's blood.... At the mention of his name the moldering skeleton turns in his grave and groans. They do not like stragglers even to inspect the burial place.... They believe that the soul of a good Karok goes to the 'happy western land' beyond the great ocean. That they have a well grounded assurance of an immortality beyond the grave is proven, if not otherwise, by their beautiful

and poetical custom of whispering a message in the ear of the dead....
Believe that dancing will liberate some relative's soul from bonds of death
and restore him to earth"

According to the same author, when a Kelta dies a little bird flies away with
his soul to the spirit land. If he was a bad Indian a hawk will catch the little
bird and eat him up soul and feathers, but if he was good he will reach the
spirit land. Mr. Powers also states that "The Tolowa share in the superstitious observance for the memory of the dead which is common to the
Northern Californian tribes When I asked the chief Tahhokolli to tell me the
Indian words for 'father' and 'mother' and certain others similar, he shook
his head mournfully and said 'all dead,' 'all dead,' 'no good.' They are
forbidden to mention the name of the dead, as it is a deadly insult to the
relatives,"... and that the "Mat-toal hold that the good depart to a happy
region somewhere southward in the great ocean, but the soul of a bad
Indian transmigrates into a grizzly bear, which they consider of all animals
the cousin-german of sin."

The Mosquito Indians of Central America studiously and superstitiously
avoid mentioning the name of the dead, in this regard resembling those of
our own country.

FINAL REMARKS

WE have thus briefly, though it is hoped judiciously and carefully, reviewed the subject of Indian burial, avoiding elaborate discussion, as foreign to the purpose of the work, simply pointing out from the carefully gleaned material at our disposal such examples and detached accounts as may serve as guides to those whose interest in the subject may lead them to contribute to the final volume. Before closing, however, it is necessary to again allude to the circular which has been forwarded to observers and call attention to some additional matters of importance connected with the queries, which are as follows: [1]

1st. NAME OF THE TRIBE, present appellation; former, if differing any; and that used by the Indians themselves.

2d. LOCALITY, PRESENT AND FORMER.--The response should give the range of the tribe and be full and geographically accurate.

3d. DEATHS AND FUNERAL CEREMONIES; what are the important and characteristic facts connected with these subjects? How is the corpse prepared after death and disposed of? How long is it retained? Is it spoken to after death as if alive? when and where? What is the character of the addresses? What articles are deposited with it; and why? Is food put in the grave, or in or near it afterwards? Is this said to be an ancient custom? Are persons of the same gens buried together, and is the clan distinction obsolete, or did it ever prevail?

4th. MANNER OF BURIAL, ANCIENT AND MODERN; STRUCTURE AND POSITION OF THE GRAVES; CREMATION--Are burials usually made in high and dry grounds? Have mounds or tumuli been erected in modern times over the dead? How is the grave prepared and finished? What position are bodies placed in? Give reasons therefor if possible. If cremation is or was practiced, describe the process, disposal of the ashes, and origin of custom

---

[1] Advantage has been taken to incorporate with the queries certain modifications of those propounded by Schoolcraft in his well-known work on the Indian tribes of the United States, relating to the same subject.

or traditions relating thereto. Are the dead ever eaten by the survivors? Are bodies deposited in springs or in any body of water? Are scaffolds or trees used as burial places; if so, describe construction of the former and how the corpse is prepared, and whether placed in skins or boxes. Are bodies placed in canoes? State whether they are suspended from trees, put on scaffolds or posts, allowed to float on the water or sunk beneath it, or buried in the ground. Can any reasons be given for the prevalence of any one or all of the methods? Are burial posts or slabs used, plain, or marked, with flags or other insignia of position of deceased. Describe embalmment, mummification, desiccation, or if antiseptic precautions are taken, and subsequent disposal of remains. Are bones collected and reinterred, describe ceremonies, if any, whether modern or ancient. If charnel houses exist or have been used, describe them.

5th. MOURNING OBSERVANCES--Is scarification practiced, or personal mutilation? What is the garb or sign of mourning? How are the dead lamented? Are periodical visits made to the grave? Do widows carry symbols of their deceased children or husbands, and for how long? Are sacrifices, human or otherwise, voluntary or involuntary, offered? Are fires kindled on graves, why, and at what time, and for how long?

6th. BURIAL TRADITIONS AND SUPERSTITIONS--Give in full all that can be learned on these subjects, as they are full of interest and very important.

In short, every fact bearing on the disposal of the dead, and correlative customs are needed, and details should be as succinct and full as possible.

One of the most important matters upon which information is needed is the "why" and "wherefore" for every rite and custom, for, as a rule, observers are content to simply state a certain occurrence as a fact, but take very little trouble to inquire the reason for it.

The writer would state that any material the result of careful observation will be most gratefully received and acknowledged in the final volume, and he would here confess the lasting obligation he is under to those who have already contributed in response to his call.

Criticism and comments are earnestly invited from all those interested in the special subject of this paper and anthropology in general Contributions are also requested from persons acquainted with curious forms of burial prevailing among other tribes of savage men.

In addition to the many references, etc, given by the various members of the Bureau of Ethnology, communications have been received from the following persons, although their accounts may not have been alluded to in this volume; should omissions of names have occurred it is hoped attention will be called to the fact.

The writer acknowledges with pleasure the assistance he has received in reading the proof of this volume from Mr. J. C. Pilling, Dr. Thomas W. Wise and Mr. R. W. Hardy.